THE GOLDEN CAGE
The Enigma of Anorexia Nervosa

THE GOLDEN CAGE

The Enigma of Anorexia Nervosa

Hilde Bruch, M.D.

Foreword by
Catherine Steiner-Adair, Ed.D.

Harvard University Press
Cambridge, Massachusetts
London, England

First Harvard University Press paperback edition, 2001

Library of Congress Cataloging in Publication Data

Bruch, Hilde.
The golden cage : the enigma of anorexia nervosa / Hilde Bruch ;
foreword by Catherine Steiner-Adair.
p.   cm.
Reprint. Originally published: Cambridge, MA :
Harvard University Press, 1978.
With new foreword.
ISBN 0-674-00584-8 (paper : alk. paper)
1. Anorexia nervosa.   I. Title.

RC552.A5 .B78 2001
616.85'262—dc21   2001016789

To the skinny kids
who helped me write this book

FOREWORD

Catherine Steiner-Adair, Ed.D.

For the past twenty-five years, in one way or another, I have thought about the questions that Hilde Bruch raised in *The Golden Cage*. In the fall of 1978, I was a graduate-student intern in clinical psychology at an independent school for girls in an upper-middle-class suburb. It was there that I first encountered a stream of girls with eating disorders and began wondering how such bright, sensitive, privileged girls could be derailed from self-discovery and education by becoming so obsessed with weight. Three years later, at an elite coeducational school, I had the same experience: I was astonished at how many girls with symptoms of eating disorders came in for counseling.

The reasons the girls sought counseling were the unsettling ones that any adolescent might experience: general insecurity, a divorce in the family, depression, roommate difficulties, personality clashes with other girls, academic struggles, and wounding or abusive relationships. But they all had the same set of symptoms: hyper-vigilant diets, compulsive exercising to the point of agony and self-injury, a tone of terror and panic about weight gain, weight loss, a fear of food, and a fear of maintaining a medically healthy weight. How was I to have any impact as a counselor when these girls seemed to scorn the most basic needs for physical and emotional sustenance, when they seemed to feel that they were deserving of nothing because they weren't thin enough? It seemed as if practically all my female student clients truly believed that if only their physical matter would shrink, then whatever else was the matter could be resolved.

Academic literature commonly describes adolescence as a period of self-discovery and self-differentiation, combining a willingness to challenge authority and the status quo with bursts of creativity and existential angst. There was no spirited search for individuality and self-acceptance among these girls, however. They all chanted the same litany of self-deprecation—if only I were thinner, if only I were taller, if only I could lose 5, 10, 15, 20, 25, 30 pounds.

Luckily for me, I had a place to take my outrage. My graduate advisor at Harvard University, Carol Gilligan, challenged me to find a research question that I was passionate about. Since at that time there was very little information available about eating disorders, I was determined to discover why so many girls were suddenly developing such disorders and what could be done to solve the problem. Hilde Bruch was the first writer I found who described what I was seeing, and so her book became both my primary source and inspiration.

Hilde Bruch had a wonderful compassion for girls with anorexia. Whereas many psychoanalytic texts of that period are condescending toward girls, suggesting such characteristics as a desire to manipulate, infantile sexuality, and fears of oral impregnation, Bruch's language is refreshingly respectful of girls, and she clearly cared deeply about her patients as individuals. In each of her case studies, I could hear her patients speaking, and so I understood my own patients better. Like Bruch's patients, many of mine who had been referred to doctor after doctor were either terrified or humiliated by the way that professionals had spoken to them: "I'm going to put you in the hospital and stick a tube down your throat and fatten you up if you don't gain weight immediately!" "Just eat!"

In this climate, Bruch's timing was perfect. She gave us a book that professionals could use, a book that explains many of the challenges of treating girls with anorexia, like the need for weight restoration before therapy and the need for dealing gently with a real thought disorder. Years before bulimia was named and identified as a distinct eating disorder, Bruch noted the common pathway from anorexia to bulimia during recovery. Her genuine respect and compassion for girls with anorexia and her ability to introduce "physicians, teachers, school counselors and parents" to the subject were her first major contributions to the field.

Not only did Bruch help us understand the inner world of girls with eating disorders, she led the field in envisioning how to treat these patients. She set a kinder tone for working with them, with her beautiful way of teaching girls about the nature of their illness. She showed them how to recognize their real physical hunger and obsession with food and also their numerous psychological cravings. She wisely emphasized the importance of immediately conveying to patients that their symptoms have meaning and integrity and can be understood in a nonpathologizing way. Pointing out the uselessness of long-term, analytic, and insight-oriented therapy while girls are wasting away, Bruch stressed the compelling need for very ill patients first to restore their weight. She challenged the traditional psychoanalytic approaches to treatment, which she believed would potentially reenact patients' damaging earlier experiences in relationships. Her methods dovetailed beautifully with the (then new) research on ways in which girls are socialized to be "good girls" and patients, and she emphasized the development of an interactive approach to therapy. Perhaps of most importance, Bruch stressed the necessity of creating a real relationship with patients who are simultaneously mistrustful and compliant.

At a leading medical school in the early 1980s, I moderated a conference about how best to treat anorexia. Each of the experts presented his or her unique approach: psychoanalytic, family therapeutic, cognitive behavioral, or insight psychodynamic. Very quickly everyone came to appreciate and use each other's techniques. I cannot think of any other psychological disorder that requires such a multifaceted and interdisciplinary approach to recovery. Many patients work with different therapies along the way, including interpersonal therapy, assertiveness training, family and group therapy, cognitive behavioral therapy, and stress reduction. In addition to therapy, it is now commonly understood that an integrated approach to treatment includes a nutritionist, an internist, an endocrinologist, and a psychopharmacologist.

Bruch was noticeably harsh toward the mothers of girls with anorexia. I too have met with mothers who themselves are in psychological agony and who torture their symptomatic daughters with comments such as, "On vacation your stomach was hanging out over your blue jeans!" "No one will want to marry you if you are fat!" And I have worked with fathers who interrogate their normal-weight daughters with such questions as, "Did you go to the gym today?" They ask not out of fear that their daughters are over-exercising but out of worry that they are gaining weight. Some parents even threaten to withdraw college tuition unless their daughters "stop taking laxatives and stop therapy!" Fortunately, such parents are increasingly the exception. There are many parents who are completely baffled by their daughters' sudden descent into anorexia and who love their daughters for who they are. Sometimes the emergence of a daughter's eating disorder can itself create disturbed family dynamics. In these situations, the family is not the primary causative factor. We can no longer make assumptions about the patient or judgments about her family. However, we can and must continue to hold the larger culture accountable for its role in promoting anorexic chic and in directing girls toward eating disorders as a strategy for coping.

Perhaps the weakest link in Bruch's extensive understanding of anorexia was her inability to think critically about "the enormous emphasis that fashion places on slimness" and her misguided understanding of the role of the women's movement in the creation of eating disorders. Bruch thought that the new opportunities available to women made girls feel "overwhelmed by the vast number of potential opportunities available to them which they 'ought' to fulfill, that there were too many choices and they had been afraid of not choosing correctly." Although it is true that many girls with anorexia do feel overwhelmed with life choices, it is critical to trace feelings of inadequacy beyond individual and family contexts. In fact, feminists in the 1960s were searching for the same kind of power that Bruch describes in anorexia, "a kind of weight, the right to be recognized as an individual, . . . to be nurtured, to be cared for, to be recognized."

How ironic that just at the historical moment when women were demanding to be freed from the cultural cage of gender restriction and to "throw their weight around" in the world dominated by men, an image of beauty appeared that is completely unnatural for adult women—the weightless waif. Although young women's bodies were still the primary measure of their desirability, the location of worthiness shifted from sexuality to weight. Bruch eloquently described the pressure and pain experienced by those girls most in line to be successful in the new opportunities available to them. Perhaps it is not surprising that when the cultural definition for success included the attainment of extreme thinness, those girls most likely to attain success would be the first to fall. Suddenly I heard fat women or simply big women devalued by the same judgments that used to be reserved for sexually active women—"no self-control, no self-respect, poor, stupid, depressed, desperate, a loser." Thinness seemed to replace virginity as the key to feminine value, and the assessment of a woman's moral character shifted from when she was sexually active to what she ate.

Although all girls and all women are exposed to the fashion industry, not all of them develop anorexia. Indeed, some girls engage in eating-disordered behaviors—occasional fasting, purging, and bingeing—yet never fully develop an eating disorder. During these same years, obesity has become a leading national health crisis, and a culture that is consumed with thinness and restricting diets is likely to become a culture of yo-yo dieters and binge eaters. Since Bruch wrote *The Golden Cage,* eating disorders have become the third most common chronic illness in adolescent females in the United States. Anorexia has spread across races and affects girls of both middle-class and lower-class backgrounds. Hispanic and Native American adolescent girls report similar rates of some eating disorders as do white girls. African American women report similar rates of bulimia, and a recent study suggests that they may use laxatives and diuretics at a higher rate than do white women. Clearly, we need to deepen our understanding of the disorder and to reexamine our thinking about who is at risk.

Feeling fat has become a code language for feeling insecure, unimportant, scared, or anxious. With anorexia, one's underlying feelings are more extreme, often representing deep wounds that are encoded in body language. For girls with anorexia, their body speaks volumes about overwhelming struggles to establish a sense of self-acceptance and safety. In therapy, we work to discover what all the unacceptable "fat" parts of the girl's self are. To a girl with anorexia, to have any needs is to fail. To be thin proves that she has mastered—indeed, has overcome—basic needs for safety, acceptance, and emotional nurturance. Since girls or women with eating disorders have a hard time believing that they can reach out to others or depend on others, they turn to food rituals and support from fantasies about thinness. Those culturally mediated fantasies become a kind of magical protection.

What is so threatening to society—and so repellent to these girls—about women's needs and desires?

Eating disorders are both a literal and a symbolic embodiment of the profound resistance to women's embodying power. If a girl has no needs, paradoxically enough, she has a kind of immense power; she has attained an almost superhuman control over herself. Because she is then unlike everyone else, she is special indeed. At the same time, however, she has lowered her ambitions, aspirations, and expectations *of others,* and has lost her belief in her right to take up space in the world.

Recently there has been an expansion in the age range of the onset of eating disorders. I have received "Should I be worried?" calls from mothers of nine-year-olds and from husbands of sixty-year-olds. It is disheartening that no group of females seems immune to these pernicious symptoms, although the underlying risk factors that lead to eating disorders may be different. For girls of color, issues of assimilation and acculturation, ethnocultural identity development, and traumatic daily encounters with racism and poverty may make them even more susceptible to certain kinds of eating disorders, such as chronic bingeing and obesity. Just like their white sisters, adolescent girls of color who have eating disorders feel special, validated, and powerful with their illness: thus empowered, they feel superior and in control of their surroundings. Little do they know when they undertake their first power diet how quickly the illness can take control of them.

Furthermore, it is no longer accurate to think of eating disorders as a health risk that occurs only in females. There has been an increase in eating disorders and body dysmorphia in men. The cultural image of an ideal male has regressed back to a patriarchal icon: the strong, tough man who is perfectly in control. Teenage boys now worry about being "buff" or "having a six pack."

There is a multibillion-dollar industry that feeds off people's feelings that they don't look right. Perhaps the most widely mentioned theme from *The Golden Cage* is "the relentless pursuit of excessive thinness" as the hallmark of anorexia—and one doesn't have to look far to see that thinness is still the distinguishing characteristic of our cultural definition of beauty. The image is, if anything, more severe now than it was twenty-five years ago, because the bodies now being portrayed may not even be entirely real. Models and actresses are often reinvented with cosmetic surgery, and then their images are further altered ("cleaned up") with computer technology.

Binge eating disorder, bulimia, and anorexia appear to be on the rise both in the United States and worldwide. These culturally maintained illnesses, which probably have the highest mortality rate of all psychiatric illnesses, don't need to exist at all. Wouldn't it be nice if fashion advertisements had warning messages from the surgeon general as cigarette ads do? "Warning: the model in this advertisement does not have a healthy female body. This image has been altered, and she is at a dangerously low weight and suffers from anorexia nervosa."

Our knowledge of the cultural factors that generate eating disorders is greater than our ability to prevent or cure them. The research on primary prevention suggests, depressingly enough, that teaching students about eating disorders actually risks encouraging the illness. Current prevention programs are focusing on educating children of all ages in the areas of health, media literacy, and weight/size/shape prejudice, self-acceptance and self-esteem, and activism. It is clear that the obsession with thinness is about power, respect, and success, and not simply about health.

For the past three years, I have been working with Lisa Sjostrom at the Harvard Eating Disorders Center, researching and developing a prevention program called "Full of Ourselves: Advancing Girl Power, Health and Leadership." The title comes from my experience in asking twelve- to fourteen-year-old boys and girls to "turn to the person next to you and describe five things you like about yourself." Boys promptly start talking: "I'm funny, I'm a fast runner, I'm pretty good at Nintendo," and so on. Girls squeal, "No way, that's too hard," or "Ask Amy to tell you about me." They struggle with the challenge to claim their strengths without "sounding like a bitch/a snob/stuck up." We try to teach girls that it's good to know and like yourself, that there is a middle ground between being selfish and being selfless.

In the program, thirteen- and fourteen-year-old girls, who are at a high-risk time for the onset of eating-disordered behavior, explore a range of topics, including weightism as a social justice issue; the ways to resist unhealthy media messages; the power of positive thinking and action; and the ways to be an activist at school, at home, and in the wider world. Girls learn to identify the cultural equation of thinness leading to success and to understand its unfairness. They learn how to resist weightism in themselves and to stand up for each other in the face of teasing and bullying. They also learn to identify a wide range of hungers—for food, for ideas, for solitude, for friendship—and how to nourish their many appetites, as well as to deal with stress without using food or compulsive exercise. These girls then go on to teach a curriculum to eight- to ten-year-olds (who are at an age when media saturation presenting eating-disordered thinking and body critiquing begins) called "Throw Your Weight Around." We hope that the older girls will gain higher levels of self-acceptance and self-confidence, as well as a range of coping skills. We also hope that each of these girls will learn how to maintain healthy eating habits, how not to bond with others in body loathing, and how to realize that she can feel good about herself in the body she lives in now.

In *The Golden Cage,* Bruch movingly describes the craving of young women with anorexia to feel that they matter for who they are, not for what they do, and to have the freedom to choose their own criteria for success. Many adults seem disconnected from basic human needs, such as connection to ourselves and our good friends, the sense of belonging to a community, unscheduled peaceful time, and faith that our children will be well-loved and safe. Is it surprising that our children also should pick up on those deficiencies?

It takes enormous courage to recover from an eating disorder. You have to dare to trust in yourself and to have hope that others will see you and value you for who you are. If anorexia is about "repressed anger, fear of life, feeling our need to control and low self esteem"—then eating disorders, for women and men, reflect a cultural dis-ease for girls and women in particular with feeling happy, vital, in control, and content with the imperfections that are part of life in the real world.

PREFACE

New diseases are rare, and a disease that selectively befalls the young, rich, and beautiful is practically unheard of. But such a disease is affecting the daughters of well-to-do, educated, and successful families, not only in the United States but in many other affluent countries. The chief symptom is severe starvation leading to a devastating weight loss; "she looks like the victim of a concentration camp" is a not uncommon description.

To call it a new disease is not correct in the literal sense. The illness was described a little over a hundred years ago in England and France and was named *anorexia nervosa* by Sir William Gull, the outstanding British physician of his time. There are references to still earlier observations. Richard Morton in 1689 reported "a nervous consumption," which seems to refer to the same illness. In his vivid observations he used the crisp image "a skeleton only clad with skin."

Yet I call it a new disease because for the last fifteen or twenty years anorexia nervosa is occurring at a rapidly increasing rate. Formerly it was exceedingly rare. Most physicians recognized the name as something they had heard about in medical school, but they never saw a case in real life. Now it is so common that it represents a real problem in highschools and colleges. One might speak of an epidemic illness, only there is no contagious agent; the spread must be attributed to psycho-sociological factors. The puzzling question is why such a cruel disease should affect young and healthy girls who have been raised in privileged, even luxurious circumstances. It does occur in boys, usually still in prepuberty, but much less often—probably less than a tenth of the incidence in adolescent girls. It rarely, if ever, affects poor people and has not been described in underdeveloped countries. According to a recent survey of private and boarding schools in England, the incidence was about one girl in two hundred. In the public-school system the incidence was much lower; there was only one case among nearly three thousand students.

We can only speculate why it affects the well-to-do and has become so much more prevalent during the last fifteen or twenty years. There are no systematic sociological studies. I am inclined to relate it to the enormous emphasis that Fashion places on slimness. A mother or older sister may communicate through her behavior or admonitions the urgency to stay slim. It is not uncommon that there is an older overweight sister or cousin in the family, and the younger child observes how much pain is provoked by being fat. Magazines and movies carry the same message, but most persistent is television, drumming it in, day in day out, that one can be loved and respected only when slender.

Another related factor seems to be the justified claim of women to have fuller freedom to use their talents and abilities. Growing girls can experience this liberation as a demand and feel that they *have to* do something outstanding. Many of my patients have expressed the feeling that they are overwhelmed by the vast number of potential opportunities available to them which they "ought" to fulfill, that there were too many choices and they had been afraid of not choosing correctly. One compared the demands pressing in on a modern teenage girl to the pressures a forty-year-old executive might experience before he breaks down with a heart attack. Greater sexual freedom may be a factor in the greater frequency of anorexia nervosa. Girls are expected to begin dating or to have heterosexual experiences at a much earlier age than before. A girl of fourteen or fifteen, certainly of sixteen, who does not date feels, or is treated, as if she were on the fringe. Often the anorexia appears after a film or lecture on sex education which emphasizes what she should be doing but is not ready to do.

Whatever the reason for the higher incidence, it is a fact that anorexia nervosa has become more common. This has influenced our understanding of the illness. From 1960 on, reports on larger patient groups have been published in countries as far apart as Russia and Australia, Sweden and Italy, England and the United States. There is now broad agreement that anorexia nervosa is a distinct illness with an outstanding feature: *relentless pursuit of excessive thinness.* This genuine or primary anorexia nervosa is the condition that is on the increase, and it must be differentiated from severe weight loss stemming from other reasons. It is also recognized that anorexia nervosa is an incorrect name for this illness, but it is generally accepted and probably will continue to be used. Anorexia means lack of appetite. Though food intake is sharply curtailed, this is not because of poor appetite or lagging interest in food. On the contrary, these youngsters are frantically preoccupied with food and eating but consider self-denial and discipline the highest virtue and condemn satisfying their needs and desires as shameful self-indulgence.

How are we to explain this paradoxical behavior? I have summarized my own observations in a previous book, *Eating Disorders: Obesity, Anorexia Nervosa, and the Person Within* (1973). There I formulated the concept that this excessive concern with the body and its size, and the rigid control over eating, are late symptoms in the development of youngsters who have been engaged in a desperate fight against feeling enslaved and exploited, not competent to lead a life of their own. In their blind search for a sense of identity and selfhood, anorexic youngsters will not accept anything that their parents, or the world around them, have to offer; they would rather starve than continue a life of accommodation. The focus of my inquiry was on pre-illness features. Three areas of disturbed psychological functioning were characteristic: first, severe disturbances in the body image, the way they see themselves; second, misinterpretations of internal and external stimuli, with inaccuracy in the way hunger is experienced as the most pronounced symptom; and third, a paralyzing underlying sense of ineffectiveness, the conviction of being helpless to change anything about their lives. It is against this background of feeling helpless vis-à-vis life's problems that the frantic preoccupation with controlling the body and its demands must be understood. This ineffectiveness was an unexpected finding. Anorexics are defiant and stubborn, and impress one on first contact as strong and vigorous.

The book was based on observations of seventy anorexic patients, ten of them males. After its publication I received a steadily increasing number of inquiries about difficult and seemingly untreatable cases. There were more than three hundred letters of inquiry, often amounting to long manuscripts, from patients and their parents, and also from physicians and hospitals who had been involved in treatment. I saw more than sixty such difficult patients and their families in extensive consultation, some extending over a week or longer. About twenty patients were accepted for more or less extensive psychotherapy.

To illustrate various points in this book, I shall use brief episodes from the histories of the large group; the same patient may appear in different episodes under a different name. I have chosen this form to camouflage the possibility of individual identification. The youngsters came from widely differing backgrounds, but when I first saw them they looked, acted, and sounded amazingly alike. If the first examples sound somewhat repetitious, it reflects this very fact and illustrates that the influence of and reaction to hunger are frighteningly similar. During recovery individual personal features gradually begin to reemerge.

The many moving stories of neglect, tragic delay, or inadequate or even harmful treatment have convinced me that there is need for much more detailed information about the illness. This book is written in the hope that it will reach those who are in the position of seeing anorexic youngsters early in the picture, before the nearly irreversible chronic state develops. I shall draw on the observations I have made during these last few years on patients from various parts of the country (some from foreign countries) and from diverse ethnic and cultural backgrounds. I have continued to focus on the pre-illness problems, the antecedents of the manifest illness. My older findings were confirmed, but with a certain shift in emphasis. A number of factors, such as the effect of hunger on psychological functioning and deficits in cognitive development in the pre-illness period, were more clearly recognized.

I observed differences in the ways these new patients approached the illness. Formerly no anorexic patient had ever heard of such a condition; each one was, in a way, an original inventor of this misguided road to independence. Their parents and teachers, even physicians, were also confronted with a strange picture. Today most patients have read or heard about anorexia nervosa, before or after they became sick. One had even studied *Eating Disorders* in detail and had compared herself to every case mentioned in the book. The illness used to be the accomplishment of an isolated girl who felt she had found her own way to salvation. Now it is more a group reaction. Recently a new patient said rather casually, "Oh, there are two other girls in my class" (the graduating class of forty girls in a private highschool). We might even speculate that if anorexia nervosa becomes common enough, it will lose one of its characteristic features, the representing of a very special achievement. If that happens, we might expect its incidence to decrease again. In the meantime, it is a dangerous illness that not only affects the immediate health of these hapless youngsters but may cripple them for the rest of their lives.

CONTENTS

1

THE

HUNGER DISEASE

"It is such a terrible disease because you watch your child deliberately hurting herself, and obviously suffering, and yet you are unable to help her. Another tragedy is that it affects the whole family, for we live in an atmosphere of constant fear and tension. It is heartbreaking to see Alma caught in the vise of this disease and unable to get out of it. Her reason tells her that she wants to get well and lead a normal life, but she cannot overcome the fear of gaining weight. Her thinness has become her pride and joy and the main object of her life."

These sentences are taken from the letter of a distressed mother who asked for help for her twenty-year-old daughter who had been sick with anorexia nervosa for five years. At fifteen Alma had been healthy and well-developed, had menstruated at age twelve, was five feet six inches tall, and weighed one hundred twenty pounds. At that time her mother urged her to change to a school with higher academic standing, a change she resisted; her father suggested that she should watch her weight, an idea that she took up with great eagerness, and she began a rigid diet. She lost rapidly and her menses ceased. That she could be thin gave her a sense of pride, power, and accomplishment. She also began a frantic exercise program, would swim by the mile, play tennis for hours, or do calisthenics to the point of exhaustion. Whatever low point her weight reached, Alma feared that she might become "too fat" if she regained as little as an ounce. There were many efforts to make her gain weight, which she would lose immediately, and she had been below seventy pounds most of the time. There was also a marked change in her character and behavior. Formerly sweet, obedient, and considerate, she became more and more demanding, obstinate, irritable, and arrogant. There was constant arguing, not only about what she should eat but about all other activities as well.

When she came for consultation she looked like a walking skeleton, scantily dressed in shorts and a halter, with her legs sticking out like broomsticks, every rib showing, and her shoulder blades standing up like little wings. Her mother mentioned, "When I put my arms around her I feel nothing but bones, like a frightened little bird." Alma's arms and legs were covered with soft hair, her complexion had a yellowish tint, and her dry hair hung down in strings. Most striking was the face—hollow like that of a shriveled-up old woman with a wasting disease, sunken eyes, a sharply pointed nose on which the juncture between bone and cartilage was visible. When she spoke or smiled—and she was quite cheerful—one could see every movement of the muscles around her mouth and eyes, like an animated anatomical representation of the skull. Alma insisted that she looked fine and that there was nothing wrong with her being so skinny. "I enjoy having this disease and I want it. I cannot convince myself that I am sick and that there is anything from which I have to recover."

The Hunger Disease

Anorexia nervosa is a puzzling disease, full of contradictions and paradoxes. These youngsters willingly undergo the ordeal of starvation, even to the point of death. Fear of hunger is so universal that undergoing it voluntarily often arouses admiration, awe, and curiosity in others, and publicity seekers and protesters have exploited this. There is something exhibitionistic about anorexia, though few girls will admit it at first. During therapy many will confess that this cruel dieting was a way of drawing attention to themselves, that they had not felt sure that anybody really cared for them. Young anorexic patients will say unabashedly, "If I eat, my mother doesn't love me anymore."

Except for insisting that they eat "a lot," they are reluctant to tell what they really do eat. When pressed for information the answers are sometimes amazing. A fourteen-year-old said defiantly, "Of course, I had breakfast; I ate my Cheerio." A twenty-two-year-old explained, "When I say I overeat, it may not be what you think. I feel I'm gorging myself when I eat more than one cracker with peanut butter." Esther went into detail to describe how well she ate but that she carefully avoided extra calories. "I won't even lick a postage stamp—one never knows about calories." Parents usually complain about how painful and exasperating it is to see a child refuse to eat. However, in recent years I have heard quite a few mothers agree with the anorexic child, that she ate quite well and they did not understand why she weighed so little. Invariably these women were preoccupied with their own weight and in a way envied their child the will power of existing on token amounts.

Even more puzzling than voluntary starvation is the claim of not suffering hunger. On the contrary, some emphatically state that they enjoy the feeling of hunger, that it makes them feel good to have a flat and empty stomach; and feeling hungry makes them feel thinner. It is exceedingly difficult to get objective statements about how anorexics feel. They really are confused about their sensations because starvation has a disorganizing effect on general functioning and psychological reactions. Chronic malnutrition is accompanied by biochemical changes which, though thus far inadequately studied, influence thinking, feeling, and behavior to an enormous degree.

Whatever their inner feelings, or however inaccurately they interpret or report them, anorexics do not suffer from lack of appetite, but from the panicky fear of gaining weight. In order to avoid the most dreaded fate, that of becoming "fat," they brainwash themselves (this expression is used by nearly everyone) to change their feelings. Those who experience hunger train themselves to consider it pleasant and desirable. Being able to stand it, and seeing themselves getting thinner and thinner, gives them so much pride that they are willing to tolerate anything. Whatever suffering is involved, the fear of not exercising control over their enormous interest in food is even greater. Food refusal, or not permitting themselves to eat as a kind of self-punishment, is a defense against the original fear—that of eating too much, of not having control, of giving in to their biological urges.

By controlling their eating, some feel for the first time that there is a core to their personality and that they are in touch with their feelings. Others look upon this self-sacrifice as some sort of initiation rite. Some are aware of the complexity of noneating. Betty explained that losing weight was giving her power, that each pound lost was like a treasure that added to her power. This accumulation of power was giving her another kind of "weight," the right to be recognized as an individual, and also the right to permit herself to indulge her gluttonous self. She was losing weight rapidly and was preoccupied with food and eating. This Betty condemned as greed and gluttony, to which she would give in only under special circumstances. While hospitalized she was grateful that she was forced to eat. "By losing weight, accumulating empty pounds, I would give myself permission to be nurtured, to be cared for, to be recognized." At the same time, she was continuously measuring herself in comparison with other anorexics, whether she was eating too much or gaining too fast.

Just as amazing, even awe-inspiring to the onlooker, is the iron determination with which anorexics pursue their goal of ultimate thinness, not only through food restriction but also through exhausting exercise. Most had been interested in sports before the illness and had taken part in the athletic activities of their group, but now the exercising becomes solitary, solely a way of burning off calories or showing endurance. In spite of the weakness associated with such a severe weight loss, they will drive themselves to unbelievable feats to demonstrate that they live by the ideal of "mind over body." Cora took up swimming, increasing the number of laps from day to day, finally spending five to six hours at it. In addition she would play tennis for several hours, run instead of walking whenever possible, and became an expert in fencing. She also worked many hours on her school assignments to achieve the highest grades. She kept busy for twenty-one hours, reducing her sleeping time to three hours. When first seen she denied it, but much later she admitted that she also felt terribly hungry all the time. But she took so much pride in enduring it that she came to enjoy the sensation.

Much later she described how during this time of severe starvation all her sensory experiences were heightened, particularly sight and hearing. She felt better at night than during the daytime when there was too much light and noise around her. She kept up her day's activities like going to school and pursuing sports, and then would study during the night when it was nice, cool, and quiet. In many ways these girls treat themselves as if they were slave laborers, who are denied all pleasures and indulgences and are fed a minimum of food and driven to work to the point of physical exhaustion. A male patient (aged twenty-three), to test his ability to exercise discipline, started an anorexic regime during the last year of college. When he began to feel weak and realized that his body was deteriorating, he increased the number of miles of jogging to reassure himself that he was not lazy.

With all this exaggerated activity and frightening loss of weight, the youngsters themselves declare that there is nothing wrong with them, they feel fine, they like the way they look, they would feel guilty and hate themselves if they were to gain as much as an ounce. The inability to "see" themselves realistically or to react to the weakness of severe malnutrition is characteristic for true anorexia nervosa; it is one more puzzling feature of the illness. Weight loss occurs in many organic conditions, and also with a variety of psychiatric and psychological conditions. But such patients will complain of the loss, or are indifferent to it; they definitely do not take pride in it, as the true anorexic does. One more enigma: on the one hand they declare they do not see how thin they are, and deny the existence of even severe

emaciation, but at the same time they take extraordinary pride in it and consider it their supreme achievement.

The urgency to keep the body as thin as possible
is so great that anorexics will resort to any means, fair
or foul, to keep their weight low. In an effort to remove
unwanted food from the body, many resort to self-induced vomiting, enemas, or excessive use of laxatives
or diuretics. All this may result in serious disturbances
in the electrolyte balance which may play a role in
cases with fatal outcome.

By whatever means and for whatever reasons the
low weight is achieved, much of the typical behavior of
an anorexic patient is related to the fact that she is a
starving organism. In classical descriptions of anorexia
nervosa the emphasis has been mainly on the physical
consequences of the undernutrition, severe weight loss,
skeletonlike appearance, anemia, dryness of skin, soft,
fine body-hair growth, cessation of menses, low body tem-
perature, and low basal metabolism. In recent years detailed studies have revealed many disturbances in neuro-
logical and endocrine functioning. Much effort has
been spent on the question whether or not these neuro-
endocrine disturbances are the cause or the result of
anorexia nervosa. It seems that all the disturbances described thus far can be explained as consequences of the
malnutrition.

The behavior of anorexic patients resembles in
many ways that of other people deprived of food. During the tragic years of World War Two whole popula-
tions were exposed to starvation, and much was learned
about the psychological effects of famine. Anorexic patients are reluctant to speak about the hunger experience, at least at the beginning of treatment. Their

peculiar eating behavior seems to be very similar to what has been observed in other starving people, except for their defiant denial of feeling hungry and the repeated sullen statement, "I do not need to eat." Like other starving people they are eternally preoccupied with food and eating, will not talk about anything else, become excessively interested in cooking, often taking over the kitchen. However, they will not themselves eat but will force food on others.

Dora's parents had been reluctant to admit that their brillant, admired daughter might be sick and in need of treatment. They finally came for help because her behavior interfered with the functioning of the family. She would get up early in the morning and prepare a huge breakfast and would not permit the younger children to leave for school until the very last morsel had been consumed. In another family the fifteen-year-old girl would begin baking cakes and cookies after she came home from school and would not permit her parents to go to bed until they had eaten every bite. What finally brought action was the mother's concern with her own weight, that she was getting fat under the pressure from her daughter.

Dawdling over food and continuous thinking about it are not specific to anorexia nervosa. It is commonly observed during severe food shortages. People will "toy" with their food and make what under normal conditions would be considered weird and distasteful concoctions, markedly increasing the use of spices and salt. The same is observed in anorexic girls who may take vinegar as their drink, or put enormous amounts of mustard on their one lettuce leaf. As the starvation progresses, the desire for food does not diminish. Political prisoners have reported that only a few would eat the limited meals in a normal way. Eating was treated with great secrecy, and most developed methods to stretch the tiny amount over a long period, one using an hour and a half to two hours to eat one slice of bread. The prisoners spoke continuously about food, recipes, and favorite dishes, and indulged in fantasies about what they would eat when free.

What has been called "anorexic behavior," as if it were specific to anorexia nervosa, such as obsessive, ruminative preoccupation with food, narcissistic self-absorption, infantile regression, is identical with what occurs during externally induced starvation. The telling difference is, of course, that the victim of starvation will eat whatever he can find. In contrast the anorexic is starving, in whatever distorted form this is experienced, in the midst of plenty, as if an internal dictator were preventing her from satisfying her needs or forcing her to reject food that is constantly offered and available. This gives to the anorexic's preoccupation with food a peculiar bizarreness and frenzy.

In some, the hunger sensation becomes overpowering and they will eat—sometimes prodigious amounts, in spite of the urgent desire to stay slim, and then they throw up. It may start out with an occasional eating binge, about which they feel secretive and guilty, but then a definite routine develops. Overeating, always followed by vomiting, becomes the rule; the whole behavior will depend on the opportunity for vomiting, almost always in secret. I know of only one girl who did it openly at home—and this led to violent fighting. Finally, her father threatened to remove the doors from all bathrooms so that he could keep her from doing it.

When there is no opportunity for vomiting, such as on vacation trips or visits with friends, they will go back to the starvation routine.

Those who become binge eaters experience it in the beginning as the perfect solution. They can give in to the urgent desire for food, eat as much and as often as they want—and still lose weight. As a matter of fact, in some the weight loss is more rapid than in those who play it straight and just eat very little. Yet as time passes the pride in outwitting Nature gives way to the feeling of being helplessly in the grip of a demonic power that controls their life. Gorging on food is no longer a way of satisfying hunger, but a terrifying dominating compulsion. Once the binge eating–vomiting cycle is established, it is exceedingly difficult to interrupt. Binge eaters are also difficult candidates for psychotherapy. The whole illness is based on erroneous assumptions and misconceptions, and therapy aims at correcting the underlying psychological errors. The binge eating adds a component of deliberate deceit. Those who have given in to it tend to avoid facing issues openly in their therapeutic sessions. About 25 percent of anorexic youngsters go through the binge-eating syndrome, and many get stuck in it. Whenever they experience anxiety or tension, they run for the comfort of food and thus avoid exploring the deeper problems.

Much of the confusion about the pyschological background of anorexia nervosa has to do with the fact that the dramatic effect of hunger on the psychological functioning has until now been given little attention. Behavior during the acute state of starvation, or in long-lasting chronic starvation, reveals little, if anything, about the underlying psychological factors. What we can observe during severe emaciation reflects the psychic and physical consequences of starvation. In this state patients are not only unwilling to talk about what they feel, but they are actually not able to because they are almost in a toxic state. Meaningful information about their psychological plight can be expressed only after nutrition has improved and when they are far along in treatment.

Marked individual differences are observed in the severity of psychological changes due to hunger, depending on the pre-illness personality, the damaging effects of increasing isolation, and the severity of the starvation. Though anorexics are very reluctant to give direct information on the starvation experience, I have come to the conclusion that the effect on psychological functioning of low food intake is to a large extent responsible for the drawn-out course of the illness, sustaining it and making recognition and resolution of the precipitating psychological issues difficult, if not impossible.

The whole behavior may be so severely disturbed that it borders on psychotic disorganization. To give an example: Elsa was nineteen years old when she was seen in consultation, after she had been sick for over two years. She was five feet six inches tall, and her weight had dropped from one hundred eighteen to seventy-eight pounds. She had been twice hospitalized and treated by behavior modification (a method that rewards weight gain and punishes failure to do so), resulting in rapid increase in weight; after the second time she made a suicide attempt. She lost again and weighed only sixty-nine pounds when I saw her in consultation. She admitted that she was skinny, but considered the low weight the least of her troubles. She was frantic about her obsessive "food thoughts," which came in "all shapes, sorts, and sizes." "Sometimes I hear voices or feel things in my head, and sometimes I get frightening mental images." The voices seemed to be in conflict, some telling her "eat, eat, eat," and others, "don't, don't, don't." These food thoughts filled her mind so completely that they drowned out her former interests in various activities (she was gifted as an artist and had done editing and writing). Even more terrifying was the continuous fear of being "not human" and the terror of "ceasing to exist." At times she felt "full of my mother—I feel she is in me—even if she isn't there."

She spoke about these sensations in a monotonous rapid voice and explained her mental state as the diet's having taken control of her; she also felt that a terrific hyperactivity had control over her. She was frightened by the fact that the concept of the future was a big blank. Elsa accepted the explanation that many of her terrifying experiences were directly the result of the state of starvation. She was cooperative with the refeeding program while hospitalized on a medical service, and her weight rose to ninety-five pounds, with marked improvement in her appearance and behavior. She was an unusually pretty and well-built girl and accepted that one hundred ten pounds would be a desirable weight for her. Even more striking were the changes in her psychological attitude. The double-track thinking, the fear of nonexistence, the feeling of being literally intertwined with her mother, all had disappeared—on refeeding alone and without the use of psychotropic drugs. However, she had also been seen regularly in psychotherapeutic sessions. Although she felt better, she knew that the basic psychological problems had not been resolved, only scarcely touched on.

Even after this brief period she found it hard to

describe what had been going on. She remembered most clearly that her sense of time and reality seemed to have disappeared. Now after the terror was gone, she was ready to talk about the concerns that had made her life so unsatisfactory. Few anorexics are quite as panicky about the mental changes caused by starvation, and most are reluctant to talk about them. Some cherish them as proof of their specialness. They will speak of the world as gloriously, or unbearably, vivid, or say that all their senses are keener. Most will speak about the experience of hunger only in retrospect, when they are no longer preoccupied with maintaining their weight at such a dangerously low level.

Fanny had become anorexic at age fifteen, and she was eighteen when she came for treatment. The family was living abroad where there had been no treatment facilities. She had finished highschool and came for treatment when she entered college. She weighed less than seventy pounds, at a height of five feet. She spoke in secretive and somewhat condescending terms about the superiority of her present state, that she had come to enjoy being hungry and therefore had an advantage over ordinary mortals.

She gained weight slowly but persistently, though with violent protests and declarations of feeling inferior for giving in. Gradually, as her self-esteem and confidence increased, she could accept her body and the need to eat without anxiety. By the time she had crossed the hundred-pound mark, something she had often declared she would never be able to tolerate, she felt comfortable about her weight and liked her appearance. She began to speak freely about her inner psychic experiences during the starvation phase. She brought it up when she was mildly upset because her roommate had gone on a very rigid diet. Fanny feared that she might develop anorexia nervosa. "I know exactly how she feels; I see her strained face and hear her say that she is not hungry, that she does not need to eat. I know what she is undergoing. I see her spending hours on her assignments. I know she can't concentrate, that however hard she tries, she keeps on thinking about food and that's why it takes her hours to finish her work. I suffered through it myself."

Following this she began talking freely about her suffering during the years of starvation, how the psychic changes had occurred in stages and by degrees. "It is as if you were slowly poisoned, something like being under the chronic influence of something like alcohol or dope." The loss of a sense of time was bewildering. Time was terribly accelerated and yet the days were endlessly long. "All I knew was whether it was day or night. There was a certain structure in being driven to school—just being moved from home to school and back home. You're in a constant daze—you don't feel as though you are really there. It came to the point that I doubted the people around me—I was unsure whether they truly existed. I no longer could communicate with people. There was really nothing to talk about—there was this constant feeling that they wouldn't understand anyhow."

Fanny became more and more preoccupied with her inner experiences, the delight over the new intense sensations which seemed to prove that she was on the right road. Her hyperacuity to sound led to continuous arguments with her brother for playing records too loud, and she felt that people were shouting at her. Her hypersensitivity to light was so severe that she wore sunglasses all the time, even inside the house. "The more weight I lost, the more I became convinced I was on the right way. I also wanted to be praised for being special and I wanted to be held in awe for what I was doing." She was infuriated when people tried to make her eat, and she felt guilty when she broke down and did eat, because it was keeping her from her special goals. Now that she is at ease with herself, she no longer can understand her conviction that starvation would lead to some purification: "One of the traps was that I could convince myself of anything."

From contact with other anorexics she has learned that they all expect "something special" as a reward for their starving, always something superhuman. She recognizes now how unreal it is to try to achieve things this way. "It's like the pot of gold at the end of the rainbow, only there's no pot of gold. There is no merit in going hungry, and you can't change life this way." Little of this had been expressed directly during her state of acute starvation, though it was recognizable in her defensive irritability when efforts were made to understand the meaning of her behavior or when she was encouraged to gain weight. Many other patients protest violently when measures are taken to restore their nutritional health: "You spoil it all," or "I nearly proved it" (being superior).

When Gertrude was seventeen, her weight was forced up by behavior modification, and she protested vehemently. "I felt wretched and disgusted in my 'new, fat body.' I wanted to wrench myself out of it, lose as quickly as possible. I could think of nothing else; my life, my clear-cut purpose, my control were all in splinters." Much later, when she was beginning to be comfortable with her normal size, she spoke about the horror of the starvation period. "It's like forcing yourself to do something that doesn't come natural. During the starvation I put myself on a regimen that I felt was very unpleasant, but I endured it because I had imposed it upon myself.'' This was a rather startling statement from her because she had been more violent than any other anorexic I have known in defending her right to be at any weight she wanted; no one could prescribe for her a "correct" weight.

When her weight rose above ninety pounds, she became concerned that she might be gaining too much; she also wanted to give up the binge eating and vomiting that dominated her days. A nutritionist helped her to calculate a healthy diet that would prevent her from gaining too much weight. To be on the safe side, she cut it in half and not surprisingly lost rather rapidly. When her weight dropped to eighty-five pounds, she became rather alarmed about the accompanying psychological changes. She experienced the hyperacuity of all her senses as painful, and a continuous state of tension interfered with her concentration, even with being socially agreeable. She admitted that her whole thinking became disorganized when her weight fell below a certain threshold.

When some time later she spoke about the suffering of starvation, I reminded her that she had always defended it as not unpleasant. She explained, "I remember now how I felt at that time, and how I talked about it. It was not really lying because starving was what I wanted to do, but I remember feeling terribly uncomfortable. I remember what I *thought* and how I really *felt*. I thought it was just wonderful—that I was molding myself into that wonderful ascetic pure image, and I told myself I was not hungry; but what I felt was entirely different.'' She described how terribly weak and faint she had felt when walking and how she had struggled to keep active, "but I did not realize it at the time that I was feeling this way." She seemed to have been disassociated from her own feelings or did not respond to them.

"I thought I enjoyed what I was doing because that was what I wanted to do. I remember I was really weak in my dance classes—I waited for them to be over. Then I felt weak when I ran home, but I made myself run all the way. I used to be hungry and I couldn't concentrate on things. I don't remember any of the books I read when I was starving; I don't remember the movies I saw at that time. My mind wasn't focused on that sort of thing. I never used to think about anything except food. Now I never think about food except when I'm ready for a meal. I have a continuous stream of thought going on all the time. I think about myself, about people or ideas, or what I have read, or what I plan to do. At that time all I could think about was food—and I used to be hungry and tired."

At age fifteen, when the serious weight loss occurred, Gertrude underwent a curious change in her capacity to think:

My thought processes became very unrealistic. I felt I had to do something I didn't want to do for a higher purpose. That took over my life. It all went haywire. I created a new image for myself and disciplined myself to a new way of life. My body became the visual symbol of pure ascetic and aesthetics, of being sort of untouchable in terms of criticism. Everything became very intense and very intellectual, but absolutely untouchable. If you indulge in being a person who doesn't eat and who stays up all night, then you can't admit "I feel miserable" or "I feel hungry." Being hungry has the same effect as a drug, and you feel outside your body. You are truly beside yourself—and then you are in a different state of consciousness and you can undergo pain without reacting. That's what I did with hunger. I knew it was there—I can recall and bring it to my consciousness—but at that time I did not feel pain. It was like self-hypnosis. For a long time I couldn't talk about it because I was scared it would be taken away from me.

She has read a good deal about malnutrition and knows that the visionary experiences of people during the middle ages have been related to chronic malnutrition. She did not have visions, but "everything was unbearably vivid." Her denial of hunger was not pretending; it was an unconscious operation. "I violently defended it, but I was truly miserable. I am so terrified of it now that I think of it with almost physical horror. I have it definitely in my memory that I have experienced the pain of hunger; now I could never conceive of doing it again."

Every patient with whom I have worked and who has come to the point of accepting her natural body size as desirable, who has recognized that her problem must be solved in a realistic way, not through starvation and excessive thinness, will talk with horror and anguish about the suffering of starvation. An anorexic patient cannot be considered outside the danger of relapse unless she has honestly reported on the terror of starvation and her inability to repeat it.

Recognition of the direct effect of hunger on the psychic function has brought us one step further to an understanding of how these seemingly well-functioning young women become transformed into "overaged, shrunken, skinny-bony skeletonlike creatures" (to use one patient's self-description), and in a rather short period of time. When they begin to diet, they seem to be doing nothing different from what thousands of other women are doing. How does it happen that they go too far? Not one of the patients I have known had intended to pursue the frightening road of life-threatening emaciation—and to sacrifice the years of youth to this bizarre goal. They had expected that being slimmer would improve not only their appearance but their way of living. It seems that the *way* hunger is experienced accounts for the decisive difference, whether dieting remains what it was intended to be, a means of losing a few extra pounds, or whether it becomes a compulsive force that dominates their whole life. The fact that they are able to tolerate the sensation of hunger (and thus achieve the miracle of losing weight rapidly) seems to induce these girls to go on and on. Then comes the sense of pride and superiority at having lost the weight, then the fear of gaining it back. To be on the safe side they feel they have to lose more, and thus they get trapped onto this downhill course.

I quote from Helga who at first had been alarmed about losing more than she had planned, but then got involved in being hungry and began to enjoy it. "I learned the trick to allow myself to enjoy food tremendously. I would eat only food I enjoyed, only the smallest amounts. It was not refusal to eat; it was refusal to gain weight." Nibbling slowly on a piece of candy she would declare that she was full—because she wanted to feel full. Then it became something she could not stop. "It is as if you create a robot and then you can't control what it is thinking. After a certain point, I really felt full. And then you get tormented by this awful guilt feeling after you have eaten any food. I became tense and unhappy, all joy and spontaneity had gone out of my life. I felt as though a slavedriver were whipping me from one activity to the other." Yet efforts to interrupt this cycle by encouraging her to eat more were deeply resented as interfering with her deeper goals.

It is perplexing that this direct influence of hunger on the psychic functioning of anorexics has been overlooked. There has been considerable controversy about the proper psychiatric classification of anorexia nervosa. In the past all cases of severe psychological weight loss were lumped together. Although a definite syndrome of primary anorexia nervosa is now generally recognized, disagreement persists about the severity of the underlying psychiatric illness. Some of this confusion appears to be related to the fact that the psychic effects of starvation have still not been taken into account. To add to the complexities, marked individual differences are observed in the degree of deterioration stemming from undernutrition. Many of the more alarming symptoms —splitting of the ego, depersonalization, severe ego defects—are directly related to the starvation itself. A meaningful psychiatric evaluation is possible only after the worst effects of malnutrition have been corrected. Further, if the starvation persists over many years, the psychic effects are integrated into the personality, and the overall picture may become indistinguishable from the borderline syndrome, even schizophrenia.

Yet the hunger experience is not sufficient fully to explain the development of anorexia nervosa. Most people will do anything and everything to relieve the pain of hunger. Anorexics get caught in this process because in some strange way it fulfills their urgent desire to be special and outstanding. It is not a disease that just happens or befalls a girl; she is always a very active participant in the process. To understand this, the interpersonal disturbances and developmental deficiencies that precede the illness need to be recognized.

2

Sparrow
in a Cage

When Ida went home for the summer vacation after
her freshman year at college, she was in considerably
better health than when she came to me for treatment
a year ago. Her weight had risen from a low of sixty-
eight pounds to about ninety pounds, still considerably
below her normal weight. She enjoyed being home but
missed the fuss they had made about her in the past,
when everybody was acutely concerned about her poor
health and had treated her "like a nine-day wonder";
now they took her for granted. For the first few days she
felt she did not belong, had nothing to contribute. She
began to worry again about her weight, and felt she was
too heavy and suffered from the old feeling of hating
herself. One afternoon while walking on the beach with
the sun behind her, she had a definite feeling that she
would be happy if she looked like her shadow, narrow
and elongated. She was so unhappy about not looking
that thin that she began to cry. She began thinking
about her whole life, how it had developed.

Even as a child Ida had considered herself not
worthy of all the privileges and benefits that her family
offered her, because she felt she was not brilliant

enough. An image came to her, that she was like a
sparrow in a golden cage, too plain and simple for the
luxuries of her home, but also deprived of the freedom
of doing what she truly wanted to do. Until then she
had spoken only about the superior features of her
background; now she began to speak about the ordeal,
the restrictions and obligations of growing up in a
wealthy home. She enlarged on the image, that cages
are made for big colorful birds who show off their plum-
age and are satisfied just hopping around in the cage.
She felt she was quite different, like a sparrow, inconspicuous and energetic, who wants to fly around and
take off on its own, who is not made for a cage.

Many anorexics express themselves in similar ways,
even in much the same imagery, that their whole life
had been an ordeal of wanting to live up to the expectations of their families, always fearing they were not
good enough in comparison with others and, therefore,
disappointing failures. This dramatic dissatisfaction is a
core issue in anorexia nervosa, and it precedes the concern with weight and dieting. The underlying anguish
and discontent stand in contrast to the fact that these
girls come from homes that make a good first impression. Everything a girl can need for her physical well-
being and intellectual development has been provided.
The parents describe their marriages as stable and there
are few broken homes. In the last fifty cases I have observed, there were only two divorces before the onset of
the anorexia and one couple spoke of marital difficulties. In one family the mother had died several years
before the onset of the illness, and in another the father
(both his wife and daughter spoke in idolizing terms of
their happiness before his death).

The Golden Cage

Most anorexic girls come from upper-middle-class and upper-class homes; financial achievement and social position are often high. The relatively few homes of lower-middle-class or lower-class rating were upwardly mobile and success-oriented. The anorexic daughter of a postal clerk had two older brothers, one a physician, the other a lawyer, who felt they owed their accomplishments to the driving encouragement from their mother. Another girl, the daughter of a blue-collar worker, was the only child in an extended family group, and everybody had contributed to prepare her for a special career.

These families were of small size; in my last fifty cases, the average number of children was 2.8. The age of the parents at the time of birth of the anorexic child was rather high: thirty-eight years the average for the fathers, the oldest being fifty-four; and thirty-two for the mothers, with forty-three as the highest age. The few only children had parents who married late and who were well along in middle age when their one child was born. Sexual relations were often at low ebb or had ceased altogether.

A conspicuous feature of these families was the paucity of sons. More than two thirds of these families had daughters only. Most denied that this posed any problems, though one mother became so depressed for having given birth to a fourth daughter, having disappointed her husband by not giving him a son, that the father had to take care of the little girl; he raised her with the precision of his professional training as an electrical engineer. In another case the patient was convinced that not having a son had not been a problem for her father, that he took pride in his daughters, that he treated them intellectually as sons; he was particularly proud that they all knew how to throw a ball "correctly" (namely, like a boy). The anorexic girls who had brothers were often the youngest child, a few times with two or three older brothers; throughout childhood they had tried to keep up with their brothers' activities. Other anorexic girls were considerably older than a late-born brother. It is significant that the fathers value their daughters for their intellectual brillance and athletic achievements; rarely if ever do they pay attention to their appearance as they grow into womanhood, though they will criticize them for becoming plump.

The question is what goes on in these seemingly well-functioning and well-off families so that the girls grow up deficient in self-esteem, unable to meet and enjoy the new opportunities of adolescence and adulthood? A common feature is that these children believe they must prove something about their parents, that it is their task to make them feel good, successful, and superior. Yet the very success of the parents, their lavish style of living and all the material and cultural advantages, are experienced by these children as excessive demands. In talking about the obligations of growing up in a wealthy family, Ida of the golden cage used the image, "If you are born the son of a king, then you are condemned to be very special—you, too, have to become a king." She spoke with anguish about the burden of privilege: "If you are given much, much is expected of you."

Information about the early care of these youngsters reveals that their mothers were usually conscientious and devoted, felt that they had done well and that the child had thrived under their care. Only a few had been cared for by a nurse or governess. In contrast to many modern uncertain parents, those of anorexics are rather self-assured. They stress how well they did everything and how their way of handling the child had been better than that of their friends and neighbors. Until she became sick, the child had done so well, never giving any trouble, that she was a living proof of her parents' superior method. These parents may well be described as good, devoted, and ambitious. For subtle personal reasons this particular child was overvalued. But the child felt too much was expected in return.

The mothers had often been career women, who felt they had sacrificed their aspirations for the good of the family. In spite of superior intelligence and education, practically all had given up their careers when they married. Quite recently several mothers expressed dissatisfaction with having done so and were now, in their early forties, studying to prepare themselves for some independent work. They are submissive to their husbands in many details and yet do not truly respect them. The fathers, despite social and financial success, often considerable, feel in some sense "second-best." They are enormously preoccupied with physical appearance, admiring fitness and beauty, and expecting proper behavior and measurable achievement from their children. This description probably applies to many success-oriented middle-class families, but the traits appear more pronounced in the families of anorexics. In spite of their emphasis on their normality and happiness, underlying strain can be easily discerned.

To give an example: Alma, who was mentioned in the preceding chapter, had parents who were deeply devoted, child-oriented, and who had provided the best in every respect. Her father was a successful business-man who played a prominent role in the financial and political life of a midwestern city, and her mother was a leader in many social activities. However, both parents felt in some way defeated; the father had wanted to pursue a professional career, but circumstances had not permitted it. The mother felt that she had sacrificed her dream of a theatrical career. The parents were proud that they could offer their children the best educational opportunities. The older daughter was only average, and her mediocre behavior and achievement were a bitter disappointment to the parents. Great things were expected of Alma, who excelled not only academically but also in sports and the arts and who was popular. She went along with everything her parents wanted until it became too much, and her establishment of excessive control over the body, and aggressive negativistic behavior, seemed like an escape from this overwhelming situation.

Quite often these mothers are unusually weight-conscious and preoccupied with dieting. Other mothers are obsessively preoccupied with some flaw in the perfection of their bodies. Gertrude's mother, who had been nearly forty when she gave birth, became increasingly concerned with her tissues not being firm and smooth enough. She followed many advertised remedies to undo these signs of aging and had her daughter, from the age of about twelve to fourteen, inspect her thighs and buttocks to evaluate whether the latest cure was restoring her youth. In other families the father is obsessed with dieting, in even more absolute and dictatorial terms. Jill's father, seventy-two years old, reported with pride that his weight was exactly the same as when he left college, and that he had weighed himself every single morning; when there was the slightest increase he would adjust his diet. When Jill became somewhat plump in early adolescence, he persuaded her to reduce and praised her for her lower weight. The problem was that she did not stop dieting but remained in the desert of self-starvation.

Karla, too, recalled that her deceased father had been extremely diet-conscious. There was an absolute prohibition against snacks. Food was eaten at mealtimes and nothing was allowed in between. She expressed a peculiar mixture of feelings about her weight loss: she had done it in an effort to please him, but at the same time she felt that she had outsmarted him, that he couldn't make her eat now even if he were alive, that she had got even with him.

The parents will speak with pride of having given a happy and harmonious home to their children. But this may not be what the anorexic girl herself has experienced. She may have been the one who was aware of the strain and felt it to be her obligation to make up to the parents for what was lacking in their relationship.

As an example I give the story of Laura, the second daughter of parents of prominent status in a northwestern state. The older sister had been considered emotionally unstable, rather troublesome. There was a younger sister who went quietly about her business. Laura had lived her whole life as "the shadow" of her older sister, imitating her in every possible way except in causing trouble. The sister was often cruel and aggressive toward Laura. To some extent the mother was aware of this, but she didn't interfere because she dreaded the temper tantrums of the older girl. Since her sister had done so, Laura also decided to spend the last year of highschool in France. She was acutely unhappy and returned home before the end of the term. She had lost a considerable amount of weight and continued to lose. Until then she had been always close to her mother. In contrast to the demands the older sister made, she had tried to be "a comfort" to her mother. Now she became annoyed about certain mannerisms of her mother, her indecisiveness, her difficulty with being anywhere on time. Then she became critical of both parents, though she continued to admire her father as the "most perfect" man she knew.

The father was a successful financier who was involved in several important enterprises and also took active part in the cultural development of his city; in a way he had adjusted to his position of being the only man in a four-woman family by seeking satisfaction outside the home. In spite of all her admiration for him, Laura felt he was emotionally detached. There was never any criticism from him; on the contrary, he was lavish with praise and encouragement. But Laura was convinced that it meant nothing, that her father never showed his true feelings, that he was patient and considerate because that was a father's job. She was desperately anxious that she could never know what he really felt. As the anorexia persisted, she also expressed concern about the quality of her parents' marital relationship. She felt her mother maintained what only looked like harmony by being always conforming and obedient to what the father wanted. Now she was impatient with her mother because she saw in her what she dreaded would be her own fate—to be a nothing, to be devoted to a husband, to be devoted to her children, but without a life of her own.

Many other girls express a feeling of having a special responsibility for their mother; sometimes this is openly expressed, in others only implied. For Mabel it had always been a basic rule to be considerate of her mother. Whatever plan came up, her first concern was,

"What will mommy say?" When she was fourteen years old a nearby university offered a summer course in modern mathematics for gifted highschool students. She was dying to attend but decided against it because she was afraid her mother, who was engaged in an artistic career, might feel left out or even feel stupid in comparison. The mother had expressed in many subtle ways that she considered the sciences to be less creative than the arts, and she had admonished her daughter not to waste her time on mathematics or science.

This excessive concern with her parents' feelings convinced Mabel that she did not have the right to express her own feelings or to act on them. When nine years old she was sent to a camp in the French Alps, to give her a healthy summer in the mountains and to help her learn to speak French. Mabel was miserably unhappy and looked wan and was rather quiet when she returned home, but she told her parents that she had had a marvelous time. The following year, outguessing her parents' plans, Mabel asked to go back to France, though she dreaded another summer of misery; she felt it was her duty not to disappoint her parents. She was sure that they would feel they had made a mistake if she told them how unhappy she was, and she had to prevent this.

In her college years Mabel studied psychology. One day she was rather excited when she came to her session with me because she had found in one of her texts an exact description of her mother. She was referring to some family studies on schizophrenia where the egotistical behavior of the mother is described in detail, that she raises her children in a way that fulfills *her* needs and wishes. Mabel gave many details how in her family life had been arranged according to the way

mother wanted it, according to her tastes and interests
and preferences for *her* friends. All this had applied as
much to her father, but he could escape into his very
active business career, whereas she had been tied to her
mother and had been molded by the mother's wishes,
dreams, and ambitions. This realization helped her also
to understand why she had a relapse each time she
went home on vacation; regardless of how much progress she had made, the mother was unstinting in her
criticism that she had not developed in the right way.
Her mother was critical of her friends, most of whom
she didn't know in person, but she was convinced they
were not the type of friends she would have chosen. Her
father, too, had great ambitions for her and, like his
wife, was critical of her friends, though in a different,
more sarcastic way.

Not only the parents but the patients too, when
first seen, are apt to give a glowing picture of the bless-
ings and happiness of their home, that the anorexia is
the only flaw in what otherwise would be a perfect life.
Some of this is a direct denial of facts, or a fear of being
put in the position of saying something critical. It is also
an expression of overconformity: what the parents said
was always right and they blamed themselves for not
being good enough. Nancy had lost an enormous
amount of weight just before graduating from highschool. This was one of the few families with an early
divorce, and she had lived alone with her mother since
age three. Though Nancy's cadaverous appearance was
a living accusation that something was painfully wrong,
her description made everything in her life appear perfect, particularly the relationship to her mother of
whom she said repeatedly, "I am very happy with my
mother." The only trouble between them was caused

by the illness. "She tries to be patient but it's hard for her to see what I am doing to myself and not say anything. She gets very upset and angry and tired." This made Nancy feel guilty; she was also guilty that mother worked very hard to provide her with so many privileges. When a question was raised about expressing anger, she answered with bitterness, "I'm never allowed to! My mother wouldn't stand for it. I'm not allowed to talk back or anything like that." Then she became silent, as if she had revealed a forbidden secret.

Polite behavior was emphasized in all the families I saw, and the parents were proud of their perfect child who never showed common childish misbehavior such as talking back, stubbornness, or anger. As a matter of fact, nonexpression of feelings, particularly negative feelings, is the general rule, until the illness becomes manifest and the former goodness turns into undiscriminating negativism. Many patients carry this repression on after the illness starts and resist suggestions to express feelings openly. A self-important attitude of "but this isn't done" pervades whatever they say and express. There is much preoccupation with what it will look like, what people would think, and with the image they must maintain. This applies to the patient as well as to the families.

Many of these youngsters are troubled by the question of what their parents truly feel and think, but they are exceedingly reluctant to acknowledge that there is a problem. Everything Olga had to say about her family was the highest praise, that they had offered the best to her, though she had not felt worthy of it. Her childhood had been a continuous effort to please her parents, never to warrant any blame or criticism. As she remembered it, she never was punished, but she lived in constant fear of punishment because she never knew what her parents really thought behind their pleasant and approving front. There was never any argument between them, and they seemed to get along well enough, but as a child Olga was continuously worried about what they felt, in particular her father, who never expressed emotions; she knew this had also puzzled the older children. Olga's solution was to be more perfect than any parent could possibly expect a child to be, and to hide all signs of anger and rebelliousness. She formed a completely unrealistic picture of what her life should be like, was preoccupied with what people thought about her, and dreaded society's verdict. Her parents were loving and deeply devoted to their late-born child, and had encouraged her in all her interests. Although puzzled by her lack of self-assertion, they were still not sufficiently concerned to recognize it as abnormal submission.

Appearances and good behavior are not the only areas in which too much is expected from these youngsters. There is also much emphasis on academic achievement, and they are sent to the best schools and given broad cultural exposure. They are taken to concerts and museums at an early age, are included to some extent in the active social life of their parents, and many travel abroad. The parents take pride in their children's achievements. One girl could list on her college application a whole page of rewards for special activities; each one, be it social work, athletics, or artistic achievement, had been pursued in an effort to please her father. Another remembered her father's teasing as painful, in his sarcastic remarks that she did not bring home as many prizes as her older brother had.

Karla had this rather touching memory. Her father had not been involved in the details of the children's education, though he took a benevolent interest in their doing well in school. Karla remembered, with affection and sadness, the expression of great satisfaction and pride on her father's face when her brother received the highest prize from his demanding school. Toward her very good report card he showed his usual kind interest. It became Karla's absorbing ambition that one day she would do something so outstanding that it would elicit the same expression of great satisfaction— only she never achieved it, because her father died a year later. Throughout her treatment she emphasized, "If he had lived, I wouldn't have needed to become sick. I could have felt his pride in me in other ways."

The describable problems leading up to the illness which the parents might have recognized as warning signs are of a rather subtle nature. In recent years parents often have read popular reports on anorexia nervosa which emphasize the importance of family problems. Fortunately most go along with the need for exploring and clarifying the hidden, underlying problems that lead them to expect too much from at least one of their children. A common feature is that the future patient was not seen or acknowledged as an individual in her own right, but was valued mainly as someone who would make the life and experiences of the parents more satisfying and complete. Such expectations do not preclude a relationship of great warmth and affection. Usually clinging attachment and a peculiarly intense sharing of ideas and feelings develop. When seen together as a family, it is rare that any one member speaks in direct terms about his or her own ideas and feelings. Each one seems to know what the other feels and truly means, at the same time disqualifying what the other has said. I have called this style of communication a "confusion of pronouns" because one never knows in whose name anyone is speaking. Father will explain what mother really means, and mother is sure that she must correct what daughter says she thinks, and daughter in turn will explain the parents. Siblings usually manage to stay out of this enmeshment, finding satisfaction among each other or outside the home, but leaving the anorexic child, whom they generally dislike as the goody-goody she is, isolated, a sacrifice to the parents' needs.

The question is what makes parents use a child in this way. It is important for the therapist to expose their concealed dissatisfactions and disappointments. Some will deny, or even violently protest, that such factors could have played a role in their family. The whole evaluation is complicated by the fact that the illness has such an enormous disruptive impact on a family. Parents refuse to be blamed and expect the patient to feel guilty for causing them so much unhappiness and worry. Paula's father opened the first interview by pointing to his daughter: "She has the anorexia, let her explain why she has it." When certain marital problems came into the open, he brushed their importance aside: "I can't see that has anything to do with her being sick." Actually it was clearer than in most cases that they were related to Paula's abnormal development. Even as a child she had felt that her parents were "different." They were older than most, and she had learned quite early that it was her task in life to give her mother the satisfaction she seemed to be missing in her marriage. When very young, Paula took pride in being so close to her mother, that they both knew at all times what the other was thinking. She had received much love, attention, and stimulation from her parents and their many friends.

Through kindergarten and school Paula was afraid of the other children. She became more outgoing in the second grade and felt on an equal footing with her friends, though none could ever be as close as she and mother had been. Then she became aware that something had gone wrong between her parents, because her mother suddenly changed back to the way she used to behave when Paula was much younger, re-creating the former closeness. She made many claims on Paula's time and acted as if she felt left out when Paula did things on her own. Instead of encouraging her to have friends, she would criticize or belittle them and their families, and Paula again began to feel different from the other girls. She became anorexic at age fifteen, after her parents had shown their disapproval of her last remaining friend.

Once the anorexia has developed, parents complain that their whole life and every relationship have changed. Instead of quiet harmony there is now open fighting, angry outbursts, mutual blame and recrimination. Few conditions evoke such severe emotional reactions as voluntary and defiant food refusal; the coercive strength of hunger strikes is well known. A characteristic power struggle develops, with the parents trying to force the child to eat; she responds with angry refusal or deceitful manipulations, such as pretended eating, secretly disposing of the food, or vomiting what has been forced down.

Actually this stressful and noisy struggle after the illness has become manifest is only an exaggeration of what was there all the time. An imbalance of power has

existed throughout the child's life. The child's agreeable compliance conceals the fact that she had been
deprived by her parents of the right to live her own
life. The parents had taken it for granted that it was
their task to make all plans and decisions, to direct the
child in every respect. These parents speak with conviction of their approach to life as right, normal, and desirable, and of their being entitled to expect that this
child will fulfill their dreams and wishes. The child's
inability for constructive self-assertion and the associated deficits in personality development are the outcome
of interactional patterns that began early in life. The
parents' unawareness that they have exercised such excessive control over the child and their inability to let
go of it are part of the on-going pattern that sustains
the illness.

3

THE PERFECT CHILDHOOD

"Every one of her teachers told me what a joy it was to have her in her room." With this sentence the mother of an eighteen-year-old anorexic girl began the interview. Another brought a note from the teacher of her twelve-year-old anorexic daughter, "A sweeter, smarter little lady would be difficult to find." They, and many other parents, value such testimonials because they support their own convictions that the miserable, angry, and desperate patient had been the best, brightest, sweetest, most obedient, and most cooperative child ever. Many parents will state without hesitation that this child had been superior to her siblings, had given more satisfaction, and had made them feel secure in their capacities as parents. This is the child with whom they had enjoyed contact and could express their love and devotion. Fathers speak with pride about the excellent athletic performance and great intellectual interest of their anorexic daughters. Parents find it difficult to believe that their loving, devoted, well-behaved child has been living with great anguish and strain.

Yet in their own descriptions, most of these girls had experienced childhood as full of anxiety and stress, constantly concerned with being found wanting, not being good enough, not living up to "expectations," in danger of losing their parents' love and consideration. Until the illness became obvious, they made every effort to conceal their discontent and were reassuring to their parents by acting and behaving as if they were happy. In endless repetition anorexic girls speak about having felt "undeserving," "unworthy," and "ungrateful." Their common complaint is that they received too many privileges and felt burdened by the task of living up to the obligation of such specialness. They become preoccupied with the discrepancy between what they felt they deserved and what was given to them, and they turn exceedingly frugal, even self-punishing, because they think they never can repay the debt of their parents' generosity.

The enigma of anorexia nervosa is how successful and well-functioning families fail to transmit an adequate sense of confidence and self-value to these children. They grow up confused in their concepts about the body and its functions and deficient in their sense of identity, autonomy, and control. In many ways they feel and behave as if they had no independent rights, that neither their body nor their actions are self-directed, or not even their own. They misperceive or misinterpret their bodily sensations; they do not see themselves realistically, and they suffer from an all-pervasive conviction of being ineffective, of having no control over their own life or their relations to others. In spite of the various individual features, these symptoms are characteristic of anorexia nervosa and can be traced to experiences early in life. The way they misuse the eating functions, their common fear of having no control over their eating, quite obviously means that the hunger awareness has developed in an inappropriate way.

There is no doubt that these children were well-cared-for physically, materially, and educationally. The difficulties or shortcomings lie in the pattern of interaction, that all these good things were bestowed without being specifically geared to the child's own needs or desires. In modern thinking on child psychology, the infant's own contribution to his development should be considered from birth on. In order to develop a reliable sense of his own identity and the capacity to express himself effectively, it is important that the clues coming from the infant, in the biological field as well as in the intellectual, social, and emotional areas, are correctly recognized and appropriately responded to. Without such confirmation and reinforcement of these initially rather undifferentiated expressions of need, there is danger that the child will grow up perplexed and will be inaccurate in differentiating between various bodily sensations and emotional or interpersonal experiences. He might even be confused about whether a sensation or impulse originates inside himself or comes from the outside. He may not feel truly separated from others, or he may feel helpless under the influence of internal urges or external demands.

This applies to all areas of development. How it works can be observed in the feeding situation. An observant mother will offer food when the child's cry and behavior indicate a need for it, and thus a child will gradually learn to recognize "hunger" as a sensation distinct from other kinds of need. If, on the other hand, a mother's reaction is continuously inappropriate, neglectful (not feeding when hungry) or oversolicitous (feeding upon any sign of discomfort), the child will fail to learn to discriminate between being hungry or sated, or between hunger and some other discomfort or tension. At the extremes, one finds the grotesquely obese person who is haunted by the fear of starvation and the emaciated anorexic who is oblivious, or claims to be oblivious, to the pangs of hunger and other painful consequences of severe undernutrition. In the background of anorexic youngsters, one finds with great regularity that child-initiated clues had not been acknowledged or confirmed. In these families, growth and development are conceived of as the accomplishment of the parents, not of the child.

The early feeding histories of many anorexic patients, when reconstructed in detail, are often conspicuously bland. Many mothers feel there is nothing to report; the child never gave any trouble, ate exactly what was put before her. Others will recall that they always anticipated the child's needs, never permitted her to feel "hungry," or that they were the envy of their friends and neighbors because their child did not fuss about food and was quite obedient during the classic "period of resistance." This good behavior was reported for other areas too: cleanliness, no rough play or destructive behavior, and no disobedience or talking back.

This seems to be the leitmotif. Most mothers state, "Everything was fine; she never gave any trouble." Robin's mother, an unusually sensitive and observant woman who had several grandchildren at the time we reviewed her daughter's development, was asked whether there had been anything unusual in the girl's early life: "She wouldn't cry when she woke up. She patiently waited until we came and picked her up." Robin herself recalled having asked, "How long must I nap?", accepting whatever time was given; she didn't dare let it be known when she had finished napping. Apparently nobody ever told her, "Just call when you wake up." During therapy with Robin it was learned that she had always been in awe of an older sister with whom she shared her room, and of a housekeeper who communicated in many ways that a little child must not get in the way and make extra demands. These messages were so subtle that they escaped the mother's attention.

For Sandy, as for many others, to please and not to give offense had been a basic rule of life. She remembered with anguish the way food was served. She felt it was forced on her, but she never protested. There was a strict rule, "clean up your plate," even though she had had no say in how big the portions were and whether she liked the food or not. The horror of eating beyond the state of satiety stayed with her and played an important role in her anorexic behavior. As things improved she still suffered from the fear of eating too much, because she felt that the early training had left her without the capacity for true regulation. Sandy had been raised by a nurse, and the mother reported that she herself had been intimidated by this nurse, who claimed she knew exactly what a baby needed and fed her accordingly. Sandy had grown up in a home with many elaborate rules. She had a difficult time in differentiating the old childhood rules from what would be appropriate behavior now that she was grown up. For instance, to show anger or any disagreement directly was outside her range of experience. She never had raised her voice and, except for her brother who had dared to shout at the governess, nobody else ever had.

On first encounter anorexics who absolutely refuse any suggestion to eat and relax give the impression of great stamina, pride, and stubbornness. This impression is replaced, on closer contact, by the picture of under- lying ineffectiveness, inability to make decisions, and constant fear of not being respected or rated high enough. These youngsters appear to have no conviction of their own inner substance and value, and are pre- occupied with satisfying the image others have of them. The whole childhood of the eventual anorexic is in- fused by the need to outguess others and to do what they think the others expect her to do.

Thus it happens that something as pleasant as re- ceiving gifts may play a peculiarly confusing, even stressful, role in their lives. They feel they do not de- serve gifts; nor do they know what they want or how to say so. Tessa had grown up as the youngest child in a wealthy family, and her parents had always been very kind and generous to her. She had never expressed wishes about presents, or in making decisions, but had always gone along with what her mother had planned. "I always did what was expected; mother planned every- thing." Several times she was sent to a boarding school, each time coming back depressed and disappointed— and, the last time, anorexic. It had never occurred to her to protest going away to a school she didn't like.

She was baffled when asked whether there were things she truly had liked or would have wanted. She couldn't tell the difference; there never had been any talk about whether she liked or disliked anything. When the question was formulated as, "Maybe what one likes is not always practical, or it may even be fool- ish," her face lit up. "Yes, I once wanted something I knew was silly—but I felt I wanted it and I knew *I* wanted it; mother would never have thought of it." With much hesitation she revealed what it was: a baby elephant she had seen in the zoo. She had fantasies about taking him home and having him graze on their lawn. She felt reassured that there was at least something she knew distinctly that *she* had wanted. I have used this little story with many anorexic patients who could not define what they "wanted," as distinct from what their parents had planned for them, and to whom the idea that they had the right to ask for something, or even to know what they might want, had never occurred.

The distressing situation is to guess what the parents want to give and to accept it with enthusiastic gratitude. This may at times lead to rather deceitful behavior. Una recalled that, at the time of starting school, she one day discovered a box containing a beautiful Indian headdress. She correctly concluded that this was meant to be her Christmas present. She was no longer interested in anything Indian and felt embarrassed at the idea of wearing such a headdress, but she began again to talk about Indians because the important thing was that mother should feel good about the gift. She got out her old books and started drawing pictures of Indians, all to reassure mother. Even while in treatment, she would engage in real detective work to find out what her parents had planned and then to find subtle ways of letting them know that this was what she wanted.

This pattern can be observed with amazing frequency. Vera was convinced that a child's task was to make her parents feel good for what they had chosen, and to be grateful and cheerful about it, even though she might have liked something entirely different; to express that would be ungrateful or might disappoint them. Fortunately, a few gifts stood out as truly satisfying and pleasing because she was sure they were truly meant for *her.* Her father's profession involved foreign travel, and nothing made her feel more reassured than the dolls he brought back in his briefcase. They proved that he had thought of her while abroad.

As an aside I should like to mention Wendy, who remembered her great desire for a large, cuddly doll that she could take care of as if it were a real baby. She had many beautifully dressed dolls brought to her as gifts by the many visitors from foreign countries who came to her home. They meant nothing to her when she was a child; she could not really play with them. Her mother commented on this fact, but she didn't dare express her wish for the large baby doll; she knew it would be rated as too childish or vulgar.

These episodes express more than attitudes toward receiving gifts. They illustrate the oversubmissiveness, abnormal considerateness, and lack of self-assertion characteristic of anorexics. Deficient in their sense of autonomy, they have difficulties in making their own judgments and opinions. Having always done what they had been drilled to do, they could not test their own capacities. Throughout childhood they "marched to a different drummer," a drummer who kept them tied later to the values and convictions of early thinking.

We have learned from Piaget that the capacity to think, conceptual development, goes through definite stages. Though the potential for this step-by-step development is inherent in the human endowment, for appropriate maturation it needs an encouraging environment. It seems that in anorexic youngsters such encouragement is insufficient. They continue to function with the moral convictions and style of thinking of early childhood. Piaget called this the phase of preconceptual or concrete operations; it is also called the period of

egocentricity and is characterized by concepts of magical effectiveness. Anorexics seem to be stuck in this
phase, at least in the way they approach personal problems, and the development of the characteristic adolescent phase that involves the capacity for formal operations with the ability for abstract thinking and
independent evaluation is deficient in them, or even
completely absent.

Anorexics usually excel in their school performance,
and this has been interpreted as indicating high
intelligence and giftedness; the discovery we now have
made of real defects in conceptualization was unexpected. The excellent academic achievements are not
uncommonly the results of great effort. Sometimes it
comes as a shock that performance on college aptitude
tests, or other evaluations of ability, falls below what
had been expected on the basis of the excellent school
grades. More serious is the disharmonious development
in everyday thinking and their rigid interpretation of
human relationships, including their own self-evalua-
tion. Notwithstanding the enormous amount of knowledge they have absorbed from school and reading,
anorexics' conceptual functioning seems to be arrested
at an early level. The nearly delusional disturbance in
their body-image concept, the inability to see themselves realistically, must be viewed as reflecting such
serious misperceptions. They are driven to be good, to
live by the rules, to avoid arousing criticism or discontent in their parents or teachers. These shortcomings
become dramatically apparent with adolescence. But
subtle expressions had been present throughout childhood.

Vera was a late-born fourth daughter, and her
older sisters married when she was quite young; the one

next to her in age went away to boarding school. So she grew up as an only child in a sophisticated and well-meaning household. There were memories of being bewildered when these grown-up women (her sisters) visited and acted as if they belonged; she was very concerned about their good opinion. She vividly remembered one sentence that was often used: "Isn't she spoiled?" Although this was said jokingly and with affection, she came to the conclusion that it was a shameful attribute of a child and she devoted her life to "not being spoiled."

She never expressed a wish for anything, materially or otherwise, and she accepted gifts and privileges only because she couldn't stop them; each gift aroused in her the obligation to prove that she was worthy of it and not spoiled. This fear resulted in an extraordinarily stingy attitude toward herself. She was always rather frugal in what she permitted herself and was exceedingly modest in the way she dressed, though she had daydreams of being elegantly dressed, in striking good style. Even more stringent was her attitude toward food; even before the actual weight loss occurred, she felt it was wrong to "eat food for enjoyment." During treatment she came to understand the extent to which she had overaccommodated herself to what she had felt others had wanted, that she had denied herself the expression of her own wishes and feelings. But as she improved, her stinginess, the frightened refusal to indulge herself in any way, interfered with the now honest desire to gain weight. Out of fear of acting spoiled she did not permit herself to buy anything but the cheapest brand of any food and would eat leftovers even though she would have preferred fresh food. She would spend much time in comparative shopping, looking for a store where things were cheaper than one more accessible to her. To make things convenient for herself, or to eat more interesting or tasty food, would be spoiling herself and thus violate that basic, self-imposed childhood rule.

Only a few parents had been aware of the literal-mindedness of their children, their continued childish interpretation of life situations. Xena's father was comptroller at a university. The parents of most of her friends were professors: Xena knew that her father did not teach. When she was quite young it was explained to her, jokingly, that he counted pennies. Much later in school, she seriously described her father's profession as "counting pennies." When she was fourteen years old the students in her nutrition class were asked to write down everything they ate. Xena was embarrassed about how much she had to write down and did not want to appear greedy. Therefore she wrote down only part of what she ate; in order then to be honest, at home she ate exactly this amount, nothing more. From then on she would not eat more, fearing that people would ridicule her for eating too much. This was the beginning of her weight loss.

Friendship patterns reveal similar overcompliant adaptation to others that characterizes the whole life of these children. Quite often there has been a whole series of friendships, but with only one friend at a time. With each new friend anorexics will develop different interests and a different personality. They conceive of themselves as blanks who just go along with what the friend enjoys and wants to do. The idea that they have their own individuality to contribute to a friendship never occurs to them. The friendships usually last no more than a year, then peter out. One such girl, who later in college became quite popular, was disturbed by not feeling like her own person in relation to others. She described one episode: "I was sitting with these three people but I felt a terrible fragmentation of myself. There wasn't a person inside at all. I tried with whoever I was with to reflect the image they had of me, to do what they expected me to do. There were three different people, I had to be a different person to each, and I had to balance that. It was the same when I was a child and had friends. It was always in response to what they wanted."

Some take care of the newcomers in school or of others who are in some way handicapped and do not belong to any particular group. Over and over they endure the painful experience that these lame-duck friends gain a position in some group and leave them behind. If they have one particular friend, they are invariably in the role of the follower.

Even a seemingly active social life may be an expression of overcompliance. Yetta grew up in a social setting with much emphasis on appearances and "doing things right." As far back as she could remember she felt that she had to be the best and was reassured about it only when she received open admiration. Even in kindergarten she was puzzled when she was not singled out as special—for instance, to be the fairy queen when a play was put on. She and her schoolmates were continuously and maliciously preoccupied with who was best dressed. Yetta's mother would help her with this; whenever she had admired a special skirt or a piece of jewelry, the mother would get it for her. Her continuous concern was, "What do they say about me, do they like me, do they think I'm right?" When going out as a teenager she might change as often as three or four times, comparing her outfit to what the others wore and making sure that she was as well or better dressed.

Constant comparison of herself to others interfered with her adjustment at college. While listening to a lecture she would be watching the faces of other students, trying to evaluate whether they understood it better than she did, whether they were concentrating more and would write better examination papers, with the result that she could scarcely follow what was going on and did rather poorly. Under this kind of tension and disappointment she stopped her abnormal dieting and went up rather quickly to a normal weight, something to which she reacted at first with depression but then accepted. It was only then that she let go of her "compare" disease and began to pay attention to the lecturer. One day she reported with a certain amazement, "Today I went into the elevator without worrying about how I would look to the others—we were just going up, each one to his particular floor."

Zelda had many friends when she was young, mainly the children of friends of the family, most of them older than herself. She made great efforts to keep up, not to be a tagalong, and succeeded in being tough and perseverant in many sports. Basically she was a lonely child, who spent many hours in the basement of her home, where she acted out lively fantasies and stories in which she had many friends. She was exceedingly secretive about this because she felt sure that such behavior would not be condoned. One of the unhappiest memories of her childhood was the removal of many shrubs when the garden was redesigned. They had been her outdoor hiding place where she could hide and act out her stories. She did not do such play-acting in her own room because there was always the danger of somebody coming in. To have privacy, not to be intruded on, was a deep desire. Going to college was a happy event because now she would have a room of her own, and nobody, but nobody, was permitted to enter without her permission. She felt increasingly isolated and lonely at school, and tried to prove her independence by going alone to Europe; from this trip she returned thin and pale. Following this there was a rapid loss of weight and a hectic increase in all activities.

One finds regularly that anorexics become socially isolated during the year preceding the illness; some will explain that they withdrew from their friends, others that they had been excluded. Some express their disagreement with the values of their age group in rather condescending terms. Agnes went to a private school with high academic standards. Though she obtained good grades she was critical of the school, saying that things were handed down to them in authoritarian ways with little room for free choice and independent thinking. She was equally critical of the social activities, in particular of girls who were interested in dating and parties. During the junior year she and two girlfriends acted somewhat like a sarcastic gossip syndicate about the goings-on. After summer vacation the two other girls formed a clique of their own, leaving Agnes alone. She felt that there was something wrong with her feeling so superior to others and claiming the right to sit in critical judgment of them. At the same time, she became obsessed with her own shortcomings and withdrew into anorexic behavior. She stated openly that the noneating gave her a great sense of superiority, and she felt better and more worthwhile when losing weight.

Many others become isolated through their rigid judgmental attitudes. They begin to complain that the others are too childish, too superficial, too much interested in boys, or in other ways do not live up to the ideal of perfection by which they themselves function and which they also demand from others. These youngsters cling with superstitious fervor to the rules of living they accepted for themselves when they were quite small. The new ways of acting and thinking of normal adolescents are strange and frightening to them. The illness becomes manifest when they are completely out of step with their age group and also their family, and that extends as well to their school situations.

As we have seen, most anorexics are outstanding students who are praised for their devotion to work, enthusiasm in athletics, and helpfulness with less advantaged schoolmates. For many, school is an important, positive, and sustaining experience, the place where they receive measurable acknowledgment for their efforts. But even being praised for excellent work does not necessarily make for a happy school experience. Bianca always felt that being born a girl had put her at a disadvantage with her parents, particularly her father. Her whole life was an endless competition with an older brother, who attended a private school that stressed mathematics and the natural sciences. Though her gifts were in the artistic field, she insisted on going to the same school, and she was miserable that her grades were not as high as his. When she finally changed to a school more appropriate to her special talents, she did exceedingly well, but she did not value the high grades she achieved in literature, art, history, and languages "because it came easy." Only what her brother did was what counted as worthwhile.

The demands Bianca made on herself did not decrease with time or become more realistic; on the con-

The Perfect Childhood

trary, more and more she expected the impossible from herself. "Since I was given more [a very wealthy, successful background] I feel that more is expected of me, that morally I'm obliged to give more. I feel that I can't live on a just ordinary scale of human endeavor. I feel I have to make this world better and do as much as a human being is capable of doing. What I have to achieve is something that absolutely squeezes the last drop out of me, otherwise I haven't given enough. Only when everything has been given and I can give no more will I have done my duty."

Reassurance is hard to come by for these girls. Carol often received favorable comments about her stories but never had a reaction of pride that she wrote well; she felt lucky that she had a teacher who liked the way she wrote, dreading the time when another teacher might not like it. Even in college she was chiefly concerned with how best to fulfill requirements. Toward the end of college she had a strong desire to ask her adviser to tell her what career to pursue, what she should do with her life. She didn't do it because she feared that this would be rated as a childish request, that at her age she was expected to make her own decision.

Nonetheless, as I have stressed, the most persistent worry and strain is in relation to family and home. Though considered the perfect child, the patient herself lives in continuous fear of not being loved and acknowledged. Bianca was raised by a governess because her father's official position made great social demands on her mother. She dreaded that she might misbehave and this would be reported to her mother. When I commented that this sounded like an enormous emotional strain, she answered confidently, "I knew they loved me—I made sure they would," and then explained how under no circumstances would she do anything that might deserve criticism. She became anorexic at age sixteen; she was haunted by the fear that nobody could possibly like her, that she did not have likeable qualities. The former childhood behavior of being over-obedient no longer gave her this reassurance.

Dawn spoke in similar terms about her childhood. Her parents described how exceedingly pleasant, friendly, and cooperative she had always been. Actually Dawn's whole life had been something of a perfor-mance. She would only show the sweet, compliant, sub-missive behavior of which, in an outburst of honesty, she spoke of as "the great put-on." She had been afraid of showing any feelings that might cause disapproval, even though they might be just below the surface. It was important to hold a tight lid on what she really felt. "When I cried I was afraid I would be called a cry-baby, or they would be annoyed—but they would never show it. They never showed when they were irri-tated, but I would feel that they were." She was equally afraid to show any anger or disappointment; even as a grown-up she would state recurrently, "I'd hate to think of myself as a person who shows anger." She knew that she couldn't control feeling anger, but considered it her duty not to show it. "Nothing stern was ever said directly, but I made sure that they would never have cause to say it." Dawn had heard her parents refer to other girls as cheerful and friendly, "always a smile on her face," and that was the title she wanted to earn; so she always was cheerful with a smile on her face. By the time the anorexia had developed, the cheerful smile was a frozen feature.

The Perfect Childhood

This type of narrow-minded good behavior reflects the moral judgment of a very young child. It is characteristic of the thinking of all these girls, even those who occasionally show angry disagreement or disobedience. The deviations from normal behavior are so inconspicuous, or so seemingly natural to parents and teachers, that they are not recognized as harbingers of serious trouble. In the few instances where psychiatric help had been sought before the anorexia developed, it was when there was a change away from overcompliance, as if that were the norm; the efforts at self-assertion were treated as disturbances.

These girls cannot experience themselves as unified or self-directed individuals, entitled to lead a life of their own. When the anorexia develops, they feel the illness is caused by some mysterious force that invades them or directs their behavior. Many experience themselves and their bodies as separate entities, and it is the mind's task to control the unruly and despised body. Others speak of feeling divided, as being a split person or two people. Most are reluctant to talk about this split. Sooner or later a remark about the other self slips out, whether it is "a dictator who dominates me," or "a ghost who surrounds me," or "the little man who objects when I eat." Usually this secret but powerful part of the self is experienced as a personification of everything that they have tried to hide or deny as not approved by themselves and others. When they define this separate aspect, this different person seems always to be a male. Though few express it openly, they had felt throughout their lives that being a female was an unjust disadvantage, and they dreamed of doing well in areas considered more respected and worthwhile because they were "masculine." Their overslim appearance, their remarkable athletic performances, with perseverance to the point of exhaustion, give them the proud conviction of being as good as a man, and keep "the little man," "evil spirit," or some other magic force from tormenting them with guilt and shame.

Anorexia nervosa, once the full-fledged picture has developed with all the tragic consequences of isolation and nonparticipation in adolescent development, is such a serious illness that every effort should be made to recognize it in its initial stages—or better still, to become aware of the psychological antecedents as warning signs of defective development. Most of these girls have educated, intelligent, and successful parents and attend excellent schools. Those in charge of the well-being, care and education of these youngsters need to become alerted to the fact that the "never-giving-any-trouble" child is already in trouble, that the overconscientious, overstudious, and compliant performance is a warning sign of something wrong. In many ways these children fulfill every parent's and teacher's idea of perfection, but they do it in an exaggerated way. It is the extra push, the being not good but "better," that makes the significant difference between these unhappy youngsters who starve themselves and other adolescents who are capable of enjoying life. True prevention requires that their pleasing superperfection is recognized early as a sign of inner misery.

4

How It Starts

When Daisy saw a snapshot of herself in slacks bending over, she was horrified that she looked "despicably fat." She had gained some weight at a boarding school where the food was much more starchy than at home. She resolved to lose this excess weight and the snapshot convinced her that it was urgent. She cut down her eating to minimum amounts, but found it difficult to stick to this rigid diet. She was as tormented by the need to eat as by the fear of getting fat. She found herself eating large amounts that made her feel heavy, bloated, and uncomfortable and she "became sick," meaning that she vomited after meals. Within six months she lost about forty pounds. Her weight and its slightest ups and downs, and how much or how little she ate, became the focus of all her thinking, replacing her many former interests.

Many others remember a definite event or remark that made them feel too fat. Actually this is always only the straw that breaks the camel's back. Concern about feeling right about themselves always precedes such an episode. Anorexic patients uniformly say that they restrict their food because they are too fat. Only a few are actually overweight, with a weight excess in the five-to-ten pound range, rarely more. I have seen only one anorexic patient, a fifteen-year-old boy, who was markedly overweight when he decided to diet: he suddenly "saw," while developing a film, that his face was too fat. In most the weight is quite normal. They act as if no one had ever told them that developing curves and a certain roundness is part of normal puberty. The teasing comments they consider so damaging are in no way different from what other adolescents hear about having curves or being chunky. Quite a few are on the thin side when they begin this drastic dieting, but they too claim that they felt they weighed too much, or that they were gaining too rapidly.

Frequently the preoccupation with weight and diet begins when they are confronted with new experiences such as going to camp, changing to a new school, or going away to college. In these new situations they feel at a disadvantage, afraid of not making new friends or not being athletic enough, and they worry about being "chubby." Some are downright unhappy and depressed, deprived of their old familiar supports, or they dislike the new food; the first loss of weight may be accidental. They may receive praise and admiration for this, take excessive pride in looking slimmer, enjoy it, and then decide to lose more weight to earn even more respect.

During intensive psychotherapy we learn that the fear of being "too fat" has many different meanings. These youngsters are extremely vulnerable to anything that sounds like criticism, and they experience teasing as insults. The seemingly sudden dieting is usually not quite so sudden or so simple a reaction as the first information would suggest. What becomes clear during extensive contact is that these youngsters had come to an impasse in their lives: to continue as before had become impossible. The flight into dieting and undoing the bodily aspects of adolescent changes through excessive thinness interrupted a development in which they felt troubled but incapable of making real changes. Their own bodies became the arena for their only exercise of control.

This impasse occurs at various times during adolescence. It may occur in late childhood, before there are signs of pubertal development; more common is its onset during prepuberty, with the beginning of bodily changes. These girls react with severe anxiety to what they sense are indications of losing control. There is a general feeling that anorexia nervosa with early onset is more accessible to treatment. A variety of reasons may account for this. Probably the most important is that the act of self-assertion it implies occurs so early; these children were not willing to continue living with the superconformity characteristic of the pre-illness personality. Another reason for a relatively good prognosis is that they are still living at home and treatment of the whole family can be carried out; the intense involvement with parents can be interrupted.

The anorexia becomes manifest at a time when these youngsters are faced with some changes or new demands which they are ill prepared to cope with. This is readily recognized when the illness comes out upon confrontation with a new situation, say moving to a new neighborhood or leaving home. It may be the first time they are on their own, having to gain a position on basis of their own merits, and they are paralyzed with the fear of being unable to meet others on equal terms. Often they are uncertain about what they themselves want or expect. Esther expressed this quite openly before leaving for college. "What bothers me is that I don't know what kind of girl I should be. Shall I go along with the sporty ones, or shall I be sophisticated, or shall I be bookish?" She had no picture of what it would be like to be her natural self or to express her own personality.

Faith had been too close to her mother and grandparents, and at age ten she was sent to a summer camp because it was felt she needed to learn some independence. She was acutely unhappy, felt she was too chubby and awkward, and did not take part in activities. Her parents hoped that she would learn to like camp, would acquire some athletic skills and make new friends, and did not take her home as she requested. She lost some weight, which was considered desirable, but she continued to lose after she came home, became depressed and increasingly demanding. She refused to eat more than minimal amounts and was very restless, running up and down the stairs or back and forth in the hallway. Within four months her weight dropped from ninety to sixty-two pounds.

Faith's recurrent accusation against her mother was, "If I'm well you won't love me anymore, you won't pay any attention to me." Actually the mother had paid excessive attention to her. What she needed was contact with her father and other members of the family. After several family sessions, things seemed to improve and Faith gradually regained weight; but there was a relapse when she was fifteen. Several things happened during the preceding year. She began to menstruate, which she hated; she entered a large highschool where she felt out of step, and she disapproved of the free behavior of her classmates. In addition, her older brother left home for college. This rekindled her old fear of

losing her place at home, being left all to herself, because they would not want her anymore. She was able
to recognize that she could not go through life clinging
to her mother, refusing to face the need for more independent actions. So she was changed to a smaller
school, where she felt under less pressure to fight off
excessive social and sexual demands; she also accepted
the need for intensive therapy for herself.

In Grace's case it was fear of biological develop-
ments that precipitated the anorexic period. She was the
youngest of three girls, and the two older sisters had
begun to menstruate at eleven. The sister next to her
was very heavy and was continuously criticized for not
having the willpower to diet. Grace weighed one hundred and ten pounds when her eleventh birthday approached; she was taller than most of her classmates and
knew of no others who menstruated. She became
alarmed when she noticed the first bloodstains, knowing
that this was a harbinger of menstruation, and she felt
unable to cope with the responsibilities involved, was
fearful of being teased or having an odor or spotting
her clothes. She wanted to postpone this event until she
was fourteen or fifteen. Her determination to do something about it became even greater when a film about
sexual development was shown in school. She dropped
twenty-seven pounds within six weeks, and the signs of
approaching puberty disappeared; she did not begin to
menstruate until two years later. (It should be noted
that anorexia stops menstruation in *all* cases.)

Quite commonly it is alarm over bodily changes
during puberty that seems to precipitate the desire for
slimness. Normal development and changes are interpreted as "fatness." Whatever the outward criticism of
the body, the deeper anxiety is that, with adult size,

more independent behavior is expected. Many have said that anorexics are expressing a fear of adulthood. They are actually afraid of becoming teenagers.

Hazel as a young teenager had enjoyed being popular and was quite flirtatious. She heard her father say, "Is she now going to be a teenager?" and this sounded to her as if he were disgusted and might reject her. Background for this anxiety was a much older half-sister who, according to the family saga, had been her father's declared darling but who had disappointed him. Hazel knew no details except that being a teenager might lead to disgrace, and she withdrew from all social events. She wanted to deserve her father's love and admiration by excelling academically and in sports, and she restricted her food intake more and more. For her the issue became "mind over body," and she practiced it in the most literal sense. She expressed it: "When you are so unhappy and you don't know how to accomplish anything, then to have control over your body becomes a supreme accomplishment. You make out of your body your very own kingdom where you are the tyrant, the absolute dictator." In this frame of mind, not to give in to any bodily demands becomes the highest virtue. Most vigorously denied is the need for food. However painful the hunger, to tolerate it one more hour, to postpone even the smallest amount to the point of extreme hunger, becomes a sign of victory. This in turn leads to the secret pride and sense of superiority with which anorexics relate to the world around them.

Hunger is not the only bodily demand that is denied: not giving in to fatigue rates equally high. Swimming one more lap, running one more mile, doing ever more excruciating calisthenics, everything becomes a symbol of victory over the body. Not wearing a coat in the midst of winter or swimming in cold water that makes the skin turn blue is valued for the same reason, though one of the distressing by-effects of starvation is unusual sensitivity to cold. The body and its demands have to be subjugated every day, hour, and minute.

Irene was afraid of becoming a teenager, not of growing up. She wished she could go to sleep—like the Sleeping Beauty—and then wake up as an adult at the age of twenty. She had been rather lonely as a child and her parents had spoken of how her life would be much happier as a teenager, how boyfriends would admire her and she would go out on dates. Irene heard in these comments her parents' concern about her, and she became determined not to do any of the things about which they spoke in such glowing terms. She had always felt her parents treated everything she was doing as if it were their own achievement. She visualized how they would wait up for her when she was out on a date, seemingly happy but actually worried, and how they would insist that she tell them word for word what had happened, that their constant talk about the exciting life of a teenager had a definite prurient character, that they wanted to experience through her life what they had missed. Instead of a step toward becoming free, she feared she would be even more closely tied to them. So she kept completely away from any teenage activities, refused to go to the parties arranged by the school or to go to dancing classes, though she was interested in dancing as an art form. She attended a girls' school and her few friends had similar entirely studious interests. She had no dates, did not consider having any, and would not even talk to girls who were interested in dating.

As a child Irene had not been preoccupied with her weight. When she was eleven years old several girls in her class talked about dieting, and she found this peculiar because they looked all right to her; she felt lucky to like her own figure. However, a year later, when she showed early pubertal development, her pediatrician made some remark about her getting too plump. Irene began a rigorous weight-watching program, not permitting her weight to rise above ninety-five pounds; though she kept on growing, she did not menstruate. At age fifteen, a time of emotional upheaval between her parents and with her one remaining friend, she began to starve herself and lost a dramatic amount of weight, striving to be as thin as possible and hating herself for gaining even as little as an ounce.

Joyce was also quite explicit in describing her fear of becoming a teenager. Though there were older sisters, she grew up practically as an only child and felt that her relationship to her parents was very special, so close that they would not want her to have outside interests. At the age of eleven or twelve she went to dancing class, and one of the boys paid attention to her. She was fond of him but was terribly embarrassed when the other girls in the car pool teased her about him, particularly when her mother was driving. In spite of her reluctance the boy persisted and asked her to go to a movie with him. She was at a loss because she would have liked to go and did not want to disappoint him, but she could not bring herself to tell her parents. She was convinced they would not agree or, worse, they might agree despite their true opinion. She spent hours trying to figure out how to tell him not to come. When he did, she sent him away, explaining that she could not go and never having told her parents about the invitation.

The agony of that indecision was so great that she decided never to face it again, and from then on discouraged any youngster who took the slightest interest in her. Her mother was concerned, even before the conspicuous weight loss occurred, about Joyce's not participating in social activities. Joyce was afraid that any interest in dating might cause gossip among her friends. She was living by the rule of never drawing attention to herself, because the idea that she might be talked about was too painful. It seemed to her that she was living in a puritanical village, where everybody sat in judgment of everybody else and where one mistake would bring eternal shame and condemnation. All her fears of such danger were confirmed when she read *The Scarlet Letter*.

She was also troubled about seeing her body change. From childhood on, she felt it was not "nice" to look like a woman, that her tissues would bulge, that the female body was not beautiful. Her mother was in her forties when Joyce was born, and she had no memory of how her older sisters had looked as teenagers or how she had felt about them. In order to avoid the sagging flesh later on, she decided as an adolescent to avoid the curves and roundness of her own development. She wanted to have a body as good as it could possibly be, which meant to her to be thin. She brought her weight down to seventy pounds, taking inordinate pride in being so slim, with no curves, and in having achieved this herself.

She was very reluctant to talk about these ideas, which she recognized as abnormal. Only after considerable progress in treatment did she speak openly about this dreadful preoccupation with her body, how she had been disgusted with its normal development. "There are people with flat stomachs, that is what I'm striving for; but I'm afraid I'm not built that way. My stomach is my Achilles' heel. I'm stuck with it and forced to admit something I've denied so far, that it is an inevitable fate. I tried to control my body, to have it my way, but I have to accept the fact that it can't be done, that I will have to look like what I don't want to look like."

There are marked individual differences in the degree to which these youngsters are unprepared to meet the problems of adolescence. Many are troubled by the fear of not being able to meet others on equal terms and of being rated as lacking independence. In recent years I have seen several patients who, in order to prove their social competence, would insist on rather dramatic steps, such as traveling abroad alone at age sixteen or so. For many, such a forced search for emancipation and independence directly precipitates the illness; they find that they are still lonely and depressed and feel alienated from others.

When Kathy went to a prestigious Eastern boarding school she not only suffered from the separation from home, but she also felt she was a failure for encountering academic difficulties. Until then she had been convinced that she, "the perfect daughter of perfect parents," could and would do everything right. She had been the outstanding student in a Midwestern high-school. Now she felt revealed as a fraud. She had the desire to be a child again in relation to her parents. Five feet nine inches tall, she felt an overpowering desire "to be little" so that she could rely completely on her parents and have them take care of her. Kathy became convinced as her weight dropped that she now was little again. Her younger sister watched this whole development with amazement and summarized it accurately: "She eats up all the attention"—and this is exactly what Kathy wanted, the undivided attention of her parents. Before she left home she had been her mother's confidante and thought she was keeping her parents together. She worried that they might separate if she did not help her mother with her problems. Now she felt that her illness would keep them together—an idea expressed by many other anorexics who quietly act out the conviction that by being skinny, in need of protection, they are ensuring eternal love and care from their parents.

Some think that going away to college will help them to become more independent, free from what they had felt to be close supervision in the home. Linda found that the opposite happened; in a way she re-created her home while in college, kept exactly the same hours, even tried to imitate the social setup. She felt completely misplaced in college and spent the next year at home, attending a local college, after the drastic weight loss had occurred.

While in treatment, about two years later, she had a dream that she was going away, somewhere in France, leaving everybody behind. "It was like a good-bye forever, as if I were going to live in Europe. There were several friends, and one who had been a close friend from school stood out. She was also talking about going to France and inquired, 'Where are you going to be?' But I had the feeling that she would be in her part of the country and wouldn't be near me at all. I knew in spite of her question that she would never come and visit." The two had known each other in grade school, where the other girl was rather sloppy, never doing more than was absolutely necessary, whereas Linda had worked very hard. Now she realized that she had been homesick not only for her own home and parents but also for her childhood friends. During the anorexic illness she no longer felt part of this group of friends who were leaving childhood behind. She would be like an expatriate, leaving everything that mattered behind, condemned to eternal isolation and loneliness. There was terror at the idea that anything she had ever been part of was falling apart and that now she was completely dependent on herself.

Changes in external demands and in the family or, more frequently, the absence of necessary changes seem to coincide. In three families the mothers underwent a mastectomy, several years before their daughters' anorexia developed. Mother had thus become someone to whom one had to be especially considerate. This led to a renewed clinging closeness, in one case directly demanded by the mother but also precipitated by the daughter's sense of guilt. It happened at an age when under normal circumstances the process of emancipation would begin to take place, finding closeness and friendship outside the home. Instead these girls felt duty-bound to be helpful to mother, to stay and provide the enjoyment and protection they feared she was deprived of.

For several patients, each one the youngest in the family, the whole picture and setting changed when the older children went away to college. Margo's childhood had been a strain insofar as she had made every effort to keep up with her three older brothers; at the same time she had felt reassured that they would take care of her as "the little sister." She was particularly close to the brother next to her, three years older. She was fifteen when he left for college, and suddenly she found herself alone with parents whom she really had not known too well. Before she had never noticed that there was strain and that her mother was not very happy. Margo was torn between her loving desire to be close to her and an angry refusal to be made to feel guilty or to be obligated to stay close. Mealtimes were particularly difficult. Formerly she had eaten with her brothers; now she either had to eat with her parents, and be exposed to the strain between them, or eat by herself. The time to prepare for college was approaching and she became aware that she was really not ready for it. With all of this, the anorexia began.

In other girls, reaching puberty may be the end of a secret dream of growing up to be a boy. Only a few admit frankly that they would have preferred to be a boy. Some will talk about it when they start to express their disgust with the female body. Joyce had played with a boy in the neighborhood before she went to school. Though vague about the details, she had a feeling that her dissatisfaction with the female body went back to that time, that he was more boisterous, could do things better, was much more independent. Now she feels that her slenderness makes her look more like a man, and she wants to be equal to men, in particular to prove that she has the same stamina. Though she knows that she is not as strong as a man, she pushes herself to do as much as any man can do, but she does not like the company of strong and efficient women because it is too painful to admit her inferiority. It is easier to admit it to a man. The extreme thinness is one way of proving her strength, that she can carry on through "thick and thin." In the older literature, disappointment in love or sexual trauma is often mentioned as precipitating the illness. Such events may be followed by the hysterical reaction of severe weight loss. That whole picture is distinctly different from genuine

anorexia nervosa, which is characterized by the avoid-
ance of any sexual encounter, a shrinking from any
bodily contact.

Though the outer events or inner experiences that
trigger the onset of anorexia vary widely, common features can be recognized. The reported "cause" is rarely
if ever truly causative; it represents only the extra demand or confrontation that makes the inner dissatisfaction unbearable. With their concrete, childish style
of thinking, anorexics blame the body for their discomfort and try to solve all their problems by changing
the body through starvation and exhausting activities.
They blame themselves for their real or imagined shortcomings, and there is a definite self-punishing element
in the way they deny themselves creature comforts or
pleasure.

In another vein one may view the whole illness as
an effort to make time stand still, not to grow but to go
back to childhood size and functioning. Some express
this directly. Though aware that the way they were
raised left them unprepared for moving forward in life,
often they still have a longing to re-create the old situation. The shortcomings of the home existed in subtle
patterns of interactions and expectations, but there had
been love and warmth as well. Norma, who had been
unusually close to her mother and rather insecure with
her friends, experienced life at home as free of anxiety.
"I often had an experience of coziness, like a round and
warm sphere enclosing me. It was an experience that
knew no fear, no anxiety." Yet she also knew that this
wonderful affection had left her unprepared for living
outside the family: "This way of feeling about *warmth*
was basically asocial—me within my family and with
friends of my parents." She went on to compare this

corroding effect on the long-range tragic development. Deprived of all corrective experiences, in particular the contact with their own age group during the important period of adolecent development, they become completely self-absorbed, ruminating only about weight and food. Their thinking and goals become bizarre, and they construct weird ideas about what happens to food. Food thoughts crowd out their ability to think about anything else. They spend more and more time on their schoolwork because of their urgent need to be superior in every respect, but they cannot concentrate because food has taken over the mind.

Many show an increased interest in cooking. A certain sociological factor seems to be involved. In middle-class homes, where the mother is in charge of the kitchen, the anorexic daughter takes over, cooks for the whole family, bakes special cakes and cookies, even force-feeds the others, but she is secretive about how little she eats. In upper-class homes, where a cook might guard the kitchen, they will indulge in an excessive buying of groceries without really cooking. In one home the father avoided a conflict between the cook and his anorexic daughter by building a special kitchen for the daughter.

Opal's mother died when she was ten years old. At thirteen she wanted to go to a boarding school, but then she couldn't talk to the other girls on her floor who, she felt, were interested only in boys. She gained some weight during the year at the boarding school, but had no trouble losing it after she came home. However, she discovered that her friends at home had changed. They too were interested in boys; she tried to do what the others did and went on a few dates, but became so upset that she withdrew from all social contacts. Her excessive concern with dieting began when she was fifteen. From then on, her life centered on maintaining control. After an initial phase of rigid restriction, she was terrified by her urges to eat. Opal developed a refined method of control by becoming a gourmet cook. At first she used this to maintain a semblance of social contact with her former friends, who admired her cooking, but they had nothing to talk about. Opal finished highschool, her weight in the low sixties, and felt out of step with the girls on campus when she went to college. She left and lived at home, increasingly isolated.

Spending time on cooking made her feel somewhat less depressed and anxious. Opal and her father live in a large house, run by a housekeeper and cook. To help her with the anxiety, Opal's father had a special kitchen and diningroom–library built as an addition to the house. She had a collection of cookbooks, over a thousand volumes, specializing in old English cookbooks. The routine she developed kept her free from anxiety for several years. At age twenty she came for consultation because her "kitchen shelter" no longer worked. She was in treatment and had a friendly relationship with her therapist, but nothing had changed. Following her therapeutic sessions she would shop around various grocery stores, sometimes for several hours, to find the exact ingredients. Then she prepared her gourmet meals in her kitchen, which was equipped with all the modern conveniences. This too might take several hours. She rarely began eating before midnight and during that time studied her cookbooks to think up a new menu. However slowly she ate, and however much she tried to restrain herself, her weight gradually increased and is now over ninety pounds. Though she knows that that is far below normal, she is still haunted by the fear of being fat.

The Anorexic Stance

Certain traits became apparent during Opal's consultation, for instance, that she cannot stand the idea that something is suggested by someone else, though she is confused about what she herself wants. She is truly bothered by the fact that there are indeed few things in life which one can be absolutely sure were not suggested by others. For a while, being skinny, doing this elaborate cooking, and restricting her eating to a minimum reassured her that she was truly doing what she wanted to do; now she is no longer sure of this. It was also reassuring that her father went along with her special wishes and did build the kitchen. But she knows he feels desperate about her isolation and her refusal to take interest in other activities. Opal threatened suicide when new treatment plans were discussed, and the consultation was terminated before some of the basic issues had been clarified.

Anorexics insist they cannot "see" how thin they are, that all the concern others express is unrealistic because they are just fine, just right, that they look the way they want to look; they even claim they are still "too fat." This characteristic symptom, the distorted body image, also has elements of self-deceptive training. They actually practice looking at themselves in the mirror, over and over, taking pride in every pound they lose and every bone that shows. The more pride they take in it, the stronger the assertion that they look just fine.

Occasionally we get information on how anorexics looked at themselves before the illness. Several of my patients were quite definite that they had felt all right about their bodies, pleased for being well built, tall, and graceful. Some recalled how they had been astonished when other girls expressed concern about their own weight and did something as foolish as depriving themselves, such as not eating desserts. But within a short time, when for whatever reason they began their own dieting ritual, they suddenly looked at themselves differently, and could not see they were too thin.

Bert weighed one hundred eighty pounds when at age fifteen he decided to go on a rigorous diet. He also began a sports program, swimming a lot and taking part in games he had previously avoided. He took pride in having so much willpower, proving to everyone, particularly his mother, that he could stick to a diet. Six months later, when his weight was down to one hundred twenty-six pounds and everybody admired him, said he looked great, something happened; he suddenly could not see how he looked. Until then he had watched his size dwindle and noticed that he looked slimmer from week to week. Now he suddenly feared that he would get fat again, and he actually saw himself larger, though the figure on the scale indicated that he had lost more weight. He drastically cut down on his previous diet, stopped watching the scale, and was frantically preoccupied with becoming fat again. He claims that he saw himself swelling up. His weight was down to eighty-eight pounds when he was admitted to a hospital four months later.

This frantic concern with weight seems to be part of anorexics' wanting to do the impossible, to take pride in being super-special by being super-thin. They also indoctrinate themselves to see the world differently. Not only do they overestimate the size of their own photograph or mirror image, as if they could not see it in perspective, they will also, in experimental situations, overestimate the size of others and of abstract distances. There is a parallel between the severity of the illness and the degree of consistent overestimation. The more they overestimate, the more resistant they are to treatment. The same is observed clinically. The greater the need for self-deception, the less ready is an anorexic to re-examine the values and concepts with which she operates. The misperceptions and self-deception serve as protection against the deeper anxiety, that of not being a worthwhile integrated individual capable of leading her own life. This is another factor that makes this a self-perpetuating illness. If there is no meaningful interruption, no help to see the world in more realistic terms, the anorexic stance may continue for years. It may end in death (figures in the older literature indicate a mortality rate of 10 percent), but more often in painful isolation and chronic invalidism.

Once the extraordinary pride in the skeletonlike appearance has become established, it is exceedingly difficult to change it. Patti's pride and joy was that in ten years of anorexic illness her weight had not risen above seventy-five pounds, in spite of repeated efforts at treatment, all of them short-lived. She agreed to another consultation, determined not to gain above that point, and she prepared for the consultation by losing down to sixty-two pounds. She reluctantly agreed to a program of intravenous hyperalimentation. As her weight gradually went up, she showed an interesting change in her attitude about her body. As long as it was below seventy pounds, she would without hesitation lift her nightgown to demonstrate to anyone that she was well-covered, that she really was fat, that there was nothing wrong with her body, that she looked normal. As the weight increased and the slightest curves became noticeable, she became very modest, even prudish. She explained that as long as she was nothing but skin and bones she didn't mind who saw her naked body. But now that she was voluptuous (weighing seventy-five pounds), she started to feel like a woman and wanted to keep her body private.

In spite of this realistic explanation, Patti did not change her concept that her natural weight should be seventy pounds or less, though she did gain up to eighty-five pounds and repeated her father's statement that she should weigh enough to be a normal woman who would menstruate. She would quote ninety pounds as the figure at which she expected this event to take place. It became apparent that part of her fight against gaining was her antagonism toward menstruation. Even though she had been menstruating for several years, she had never accepted it as a natural function, always treating it with the greatest secrecy, even as nonexistent.

Deep down she was convinced that her father did not want her to weigh more than seventy pounds because he hated fat women. After the initial weight gain she manipulated the intravenous feeding, turning it off at night, and gained only three more pounds during the next two months, up to eighty-five pounds. She complained that she was fat, felt round and full and couldn't tolerate the idea of being fat, didn't understand why the scale didn't show how much weight she had gained. She actually looked much prettier, no longer a skeleton, with beginning feminine curves and a new softness to her face. She put posters on the wall and wrote notes to herself: "I feel guilty when I eat anything, especially high-caloric foods. I feel naughty, low, base, repulsed by myself after I eat. I feel like I overeat if I eat normally. I cry to release this guilt and I feel bad about myself." She repeated these statements: "I don't eat because eating makes me gain weight and I

The Anorexic Stance

don't want to gain weight. I think I really want to eat, but not gain weight so I can keep my skinny scarecrow figure. I have a deep fear of having a womanly body, round and fully developed. I want to be tight and muscular and thin. Slender I could stand, but no more." She became more lively and active as her weight increased. Since she continuously protested that she would eat normally if only the intravenous feedings were stopped, this was put to the test. In one week she lost five pounds while talking about how much she enjoyed eating and gaining weight—a complete disregard of the facts.

During this time she was seen in psychotherapy and was eager to come to an understanding of herself. Always she had felt that pleasing father was the goal of her life. When she felt she could no longer fulfill his wishes, she tried to escape into the anorexic way of life, which she now considers a fraudulent solution. She feels even that her illness is a fraud. She calls one part of herself, who insists on being skinny and can't eat, the "fraud girl"—but she cannot give up this style of life because, if she were well with a normal weight, then she would have to go back and be father's obedient servant.

I was trying to be somebody my parents wanted me to be, or at least the person I thought they wanted me to be. Maybe it was all my own feelings that sensed that Daddy wanted me to be a good student and to have the right friends, for he never stated it outright. I just kind of felt it deep down inside. It was like in the atmosphere or in the air around me. It was really a self-imposed pressure because he never outwardly asked me to study. I did the best I could, but I guess it wasn't good enough.

The Golden Cage

I failed in all ways, but at least from now on I can try to be the best "me" possible and hope that he'll love me just the same even if I can't meet all of his desires for me.

Patti expressed the same idea in a nightmare, one of the few dreams she had remembered during her long illness. It was as if she were back in highschool where she was supposed to present a book report. It suddenly dawned on her that she had not read the book, had not even started it. It was a frantic, panic-arousing situation: now it would become apparent that she was not the student she had pretended to be, that she really was not interested in literature or in any other studies, that she had forced herself to do all these things because her father had expected it. Waking up was a great relief, with the knowledge that she had finished highschool and college, though she sadly admitted that with all the studying she had forced herself to do she did not remember anything she had studied; the only thing that had mattered was to do what had been expected of her.

She spoke with real anguish about the abnormality of her present life; instead of being a grown-up daughter living at home, she had remained in the position of a child, as afraid of the responsibilities of independent living as of gaining weight, convinced she had to be thin. She felt she had not had the experiences to prepare her for independence. This appeared to be one patient who needed long-term treatment in a psychiatric residential center where she could reexamine her misconceptions, become more competent and mature, and be protected against the destructive dieting.

Those who stay sick with anorexia for any length of time develop peculiar misconceptions and strange feelings about the body and its functions, as we have seen. These misinterpretations begin to develop soon after the onset of starvation, and they become more distorted and more rigidly integrated the longer the anorexic state lasts. Since these are well-educated people, some even students of biology with a good knowledge of physiology and nutrition, the clinging to such abnormal imagery is amazing. They are aware that their ideas do not coincide with what they have learned, but their reactions and behavior are dominated by fantastic notions about what happens to food. One girl expressed it as, "My stomach is like a paper bag—whatever I put in, it just sits there and makes me feel full"; she was quite violent in her efforts to remove all food by choking, at times seriously hurting herself. Others feel the results depend on the quality of the food. If they eat junk food, or anything they disapprove of according to their value system, they are convinced it will go directly to places where they do not want fat to accumulate. They suffer from persistent anxiety that eating might stretch the stomach or make it bulge; they can feel relaxed only if the stomach is completely flat.

This has been interpreted in the past as indicating a fear of pregnancy. It does not hold true for my group of patients; several had pregnancy fantasies with a positive connotation. One seventeen-year-old girl who was hospitalized to protect her against the violent methods with which she made herself vomit and who was delusionally preoccupied with the "bulges" made by her well-developed stomach muscles (she was a good sportswoman), had a dream, which she felt was pleasant and reassuring, during the first night in the hospital. She dreamed she was pregnant and ready to deliver. She was afraid of natural childbirth, but that was the method used and it was not bad at all.

Anorexic patients who indulge in binge eating develop bizarre notions about food, different in each case, but they have in common the conviction that the food they feel compelled to gulp down cannot be integrated or would be damaging and therefore has to be removed from the body by vomiting. Once this symptom complex develops, it has a tendency to become more severe and resistant to treatment. In order to bring the food up again, larger and larger quantities have to be consumed. The sums spent on this routine are prodigious. Each one becomes a specialist in the type of food she uses, ranging from meals, one on top of the other, in gourmet restaurants to emptying the freezer at home in night orgies of broiled steaks, to junk food bought by the carload in the nearest supermarket. Whatever it is, it is washed down by quarts of milk and other fluids to make it easier to regurgitate.

Vomiting also becomes an individualized ritual; some have great difficulty in bringing the food up and may hurt themselves in their efforts. Others just "whoop it up" without any particular stimulation. Most use something soft to tickle the throat and release the gag reflex. Since they remove the food, they are continuously hungry and therefore may go on binges several times a day. It may become so time-consuming that there is little time left for anything else.

Most of the difficulties come into the open only when they make efforts to get rid of this troublesome symptom, of which they become more and more ashamed. If things go well and nothing upsetting happens, they may have a relaxed day, looking forward to a large evening meal which is then thrown up. But if anything goes wrong, or if there is an unplanned period of spare time, an irresistible impulse to go on an eating spree takes over; then comes remorse and another binge, and all resolutions to stop are swept away.

What started in response to ravenous hunger becomes more and more a way to relieve tension in general. A vicious cycle develops. The fear of not having enough food for a binge, or the privacy for vomiting, may create so much tension that all other activities are postponed until the ritual is completed. If for one or another reason the vomiting must be postponed, a chronic binger will complete the act by trying to vomit several hours later, even though most of the food has already left the stomach. The conviction that the food is dirty or damaging is so strong that they feel pure and liberated only by emptying themselves.

Anxiety about the fate of food may also result in excessive exercising. Ruth, for instance, felt that the food would distribute itself normally, would make her gradually stronger without accumulating in any particular place, if she kept very active. By exercising she felt she could send food to the desired places, and she accomplished this by swimming at least a mile, when she had time many more, every day. Having used laxatives for many years, under the principle that "what goes in must go out," she was also convinced that her bowels could no longer function without this stimulation, and she became panicky when she was without a movement for a single day.

In the long run, anorexics develop a whole range of symptoms to maintain the ultimate thinness. Such symptoms are of different severity in different people. The stereotype statement, "I'm not hungry—I don't need to eat," is followed by declarations that the stomach no longer accepts food and the person becomes sick when eating. They all explain their restricted food intake, that they cannot eat more than a token morsel, by "feeling full." This explanation is given even by those who go on eating binges and consume large amounts in a frenzy of hunger, but who ordinarily insist that they feel full with the smallest amount. This too expresses the conviction that the mind can do anything and can control the body in every way it wants. To be questioned about this during the acute phase of the illness arouses anger and defensive statements; this is just the way they feel, and some even cry for having been called a liar. And yet, when they are no longer preoccupied with maintaining an abnormally low weight, they themselves will explain their actions as a form of deceit.

Sophie had clung to an extremely low weight for several years; when under pressure in her academic work, she suddenly let go of her excessive control and regained a normal weight in a relatively short time. After a short depressive reaction, she became much more relaxed and freer in her whole daily functioning. When asked about the continuous complaint about fullness, she answered, with a shrug of the shoulder, "It's a big lie." This declaration was reconsidered and she then described how she had taught herself to eat very slowly, paying the most minute attention to what she thought she felt and how she could then say, honestly, that she felt full.

Tania gave a similar explanation, that she had trained herself to feel full. She would eat one tiny M & M candy very slowly, just nibbling on it, and told herself that she could feel her stomach getting full. It was difficult for her to describe, and even more difficult for me to understand, how she learned to pay such minute attention to her stomach sensations. Later, after treatment, she said: "You brainwash yourself—and once you start on the wrong path, then you become blind to what is going on. By doing something that makes you different you become blinded to what you are doing. This is a deceptive blindness, but it is very difficult to give it up and you begin to see it only after you have reexamined your values." Such reevaluation is, of course, the outcome of the therapeutic exploration of the underlying self-deceptions that are a core issue in anorexia nervosa.

The sense of time appears to be distorted in all cases, though different girls experience it differently. Ursula was continuously involved with preventing and postponing. She felt urgent about being slim *now* to avoid being plump, with a midriff bulge, when middle-aged. She would skip lunch because then she might not be hungry at dinnertime, and eating when not weak from hunger went against her frugal principles. Though she spoke continuously about wanting to gain weight, knowing that she could not go through life with a child's body, she always managed to lose slowly, over an extended period, the weight she had painfully gained during several hospitalizations. It was just never the right time to eat.

Entirely different was the concept of time that Vicky described. She was a binge eater and had reached the stage where she would plan a binge for late in the day. She was unhappy that she also had uncontrollable urges for binging at unexpected and unplanned times. Her experience of time was unusual; she was moving through time and this gave her an unstable feeling, always being confronted with an unknown future. When the time ahead was finite, a few hours with planned activities, things were all right. But if there were undefined hours ahead, she experienced a sort of emptiness or discontinuity, threatening and ominous. She felt as if she were moving through darkness—nothing in between—and the urge for eating would press up. "The idea of hunger is that you are not going to be able to get food, you are going to go indefinitely without food, so you *have to* eat right now." Then she would fill herself up with as much food as she could hold—and then throw it up. The distorted sense of time appeared related to her failure of an inner sense of stability, like not having a center of gravity within herself.

Myra, a thirty-five-year-old woman who had been a binge eater for over fifteen years, used a similar image to describe the emptiness of her life that would trigger a bout of gorging. She alternated between eating huge amounts and not eating at all, and her weight had fluctuated between eighty and one hundred and sixty pounds. She would prepare detailed lists of what to do every single day, "to protect myself against something that is very frightening to me—spaces in my life." She was aware that this was related to her concept of time. "Time is like something to be gotten through right now. It is a thick forest and I have to get through it. Whenever there are spaces in the forest, I don't know how to get through them and I get frightened, terribly frightened. Undefined spaces frighten me awfully. I live my life so I don't have to deal with them." When there was open time she would run to the nearest delicatessen or restaurant to fill herself up, no matter how late at night. The feeling of "space" was associated with being afraid to be alone at home with nothing to do. Sitting down and reading a book or watching television was no protection against this feeling of a terrifying stretch of space.

These stories of the tragic long-term invalidism

suffered by these women illustrate that anorexia nervosa is an extremely complex illness, much more than dieting gone wild. Its true beginning is the child's passive participation in life, absorbing from the world without actively integrating anything. The relationship to parents appears superficially to be congenial; actually it is too close, without necessary separation, individuation, and differentiation. This harmony is achieved through excessive conformity on the part of the child, always fitting in, always doing what is expected, and this is attained at the price of not taking active steps toward inner development of autonomy. Since things have been going so well during childhood, the parents expect "normal" development to continue; with approaching adolescence they expect greater "independence," but independence on their own terms. In reviewing the development, parents will say, in seemingly self-accusing terms, that they recognize their error now, that they failed to instill independence into their child.

When positive self-assertion becomes unavoidable for a child, when an attitude of fitting in is no longer appropriate, the severe deficiencies in the core personality become apparent. The weight loss accomplishes much: the parents are drawn back into being protective, not demanding, toward the child who for the first time experiences that she has power and is in control. Many anorexics explain why they cling to the illness with the simple statement, "If I were well they would not pay attention to me," or "They won't love me anymore." The tragedy is that the very attention they demand reinforces the old abnormal patterns, making development of true independence impossible.

The longer the illness lasts, the more isolated an individual becomes, then the greater is the danger of being completely self-absorbed, overpowered by bizarre and abnormal ruminations. Without meaningful interruption the chronic anorexic state may last forever; I have seen women in their forties and fifties proudly defending their skeletonlike figures, repeating the same phrases of not being able to eat because they feel full. The picture is complicated by the fact that starvation produces serious physiological disturbances that make the condition self-perpetuating. The starving organism is like a closed system that goes on functioning indefinitely on a reduced level.

The starvation has also a marked influence on psychological functioning. The distorted concepts with which anorexics operate and the ruminative preoccupation with food are thus maintained. No amount of psychological reasoning in ordinary psychotherapy can be effective so long as the basic psychological reactions are determined by the state of starvation. For effective treatment, changes and correction must be accomplished in several areas: the abnormal nutrition must be improved; the stagnating patterns of family interaction must be clarified and unlocked; most of all, the undifferentiated slavelike self-concept must mature. Psychotherapy has to be a process of encouraging the development of the basic personality and of liberating it from the fearful state of not feeling separated from the enmeshment with parents.

6

WEIGHT CORRECTION

When Willa was sixteen years old she spent a lonely summer in her hometown, refusing to go with her parents to their lakeside cottage and also keeping away from her former friends. While she took her school examinations her weight had gone up to one hundred pounds. She felt she should be slimmer and decided to go down to ninety pounds. She had been preoccupied with controlling her weight for several years and knew it would be difficult; she had always suffered on a diet. To her amazement she found that it was easy to lose, so easy that she was suddenly afraid she would keep on losing. At the same time, she was overjoyed that she could do it so easily.

Willa was so pleased with the results that she cut down her intake even more and taught herself the trick of enjoying each bit of food tremendously. She would eat only food she liked, in the smallest amounts. She also began an extensive exercise program, would walk and run endlessly, do calisthenics at night, and sleep less and less. She took up dancing—though she did not have the strength, she gloried in the fact that she had a fantastic leg stretch. She kept on losing weight.

Family life deteriorated to constant fighting and arguing to make her eat. She became weaker and felt there was something wrong, that she was destroying herself. Finally she wanted to go into a hospital in a nearby larger city. She conceived of the hospital as a place where she would be nurtured back to life, be made all over again. "I saw myself in a white room, in a white bed, lying down, and they would bring me healthy food." Instead the dietician asked what she liked best and, when she said icecream and cake, that was the food that was served on her tray; she was disgusted with it. She lost some more weight, down to sixty-eight pounds. When tube feeding was planned she was at first pleased with the idea; then she heard how distressing it was. She was so desperate that she started to eat and was given free access to whatever food she wanted. Whenever she felt tense or anxious, she would run into the kitchen and stuff herself with sweets and icecream. But it disgusted her that this was not the healthful, life-restoring food she had dreamed of. The staff did not understand her desire for good food; they just were pleased that she was gaining weight so rapidly. In less than two months she was discharged as "greatly improved," weighing ninety-six pounds. Her parents were jubilant when they took her home; everybody was happy except Willa. She felt she had lost all control over her eating and continued with uncontrollable eating binges, followed by self-induced vomiting.

When in less than two weeks her weight dropped by ten pounds, she was sent to another hospital where she was placed on a behavior modification program; on any day in which she had failed to gain the prescribed amount of weight, she was given three tube feedings. Within three months her weight rose to one hundred

five pounds. Again she was discharged as "greatly improved" though she had become seriously depressed,
even suicidal. She had felt humiliated by the
procedure of being coerced into stuffing herself against
her will. She resumed binge eating followed by
vomiting. She was seen regularly by a physician for
whom she produced the required weight of ninety
pounds by eating huge amounts, and drinking fluids
before going to his office; she made herself regurgitate
as soon as the weight had been registered. She continued
in school where she received high grades, and she engaged in many other activities. When she was seen in
consultation a year later she had brought her weight
down to seventy-two pounds and was desperately unhappy.

This story illustrates that there is more to the treatment of anorexia nervosa than inducing weight gain.
The correction of the weight problem must be part of an
integrated treatment approach. The patient needs to
be instructed, and also the family, that in spite of outer
appearances this is not an illness of weight and appetite
—the essential problem relates to inner doubts and lack
of self-confidence. However, in order to get help with
these underlying problems, the body needs to be in a
better condition. The patient is usually terror-stricken
at the idea of having to gain weight, and it is important
to give her a meaningful explanation why better nutrition is an essential precondition for coming to an understanding of her psychological problems. She also
needs reassurance that a good diet will be served in
amounts that will protect her from gaining too fast and
becoming fat. The overpermissive regime with completely undisciplined eating to which Willa had been

exposed is antitherapeutic. Yet this type of indulgent feeding is reported by many others, particularly by those who have been exposed to a program of refeeding through behavior modification.

Since the illness was first described a little over a century ago, there has been continuous debate about how to accomplish the seemingly impossible task of getting food into a patient who is stubbornly determined to starve herself. The discussion has been extended to what food to offer, how to feed it, where to do it, and what medication to use. The writings often reflect a desperate frustration, a helpless feeling of being involved in a battle of wills. The physiological principles are simple: increase the food intake and decrease the activity of these driven cachectic girls. The question is how to persuade, trick, bribe, or force a negativistic patient into doing what she is determined not to do, and how to achieve this without doing more psychological damage.

There has been considerable controversy about the merits of hospitalization. A tradition has developed that it is best to treat these patients away from their families. A decision about what to do depends on many individual circumstances—the age of the patient, the severity of the weight loss and general condition, the duration of the illness, the emotional climate of the home, and the quality, experience, and treatment philosophy of the available hospital. Brief admission to a service without special experience in the management of anorexia can create as many problems as it attempts to solve. The personnel is as helpless and inconsistent in dealing with the deceitfulness and cunning of these patients as was the family, and they are apt to respond with anxiety, frustration, and anger to the patient's manipulative behavior.

This applies both to medical and to psychiatric hospital facilities. Thus the hospital stay may be characterized by the same type of frantic emergency situations that led to the hospitalization in the first place. Quite often the patient will eat and gain weight in order to get out of the hospital—and then will lose again. If a daytime nurse succeeds in developing an understanding attitude toward the patient's needs, it will happen over and over that a substitute night nurse will blunder and threaten a patient with dire consequences if she doesn't follow her instructions. On the other hand, if the nurses and dieticians are experienced and show consistent warm understanding for the patient's plight, weight gain in a hospital setting may be a beneficial experience, a direct aid in regaining her health, and also an interruption of the tension that may have risen to panic level in the family.

Living away from home may be accomplished in various ways. Some of the young patients I have seen had been sent to boarding schools. If left without psychiatric help, the condition is apt to get worse. College, too, does not offer a cure; on the contrary, many became anorexic when going away to college was the first separation from home. On the other hand, for those who are in psychiatric treatment, a college dormitory offers a convenient place to live. It is not as isolated as living alone in an apartment; companionship is available but not as intrusive as in family life. If there is more than one anorexic in a dormitory, interesting relationships develop which may be initially competitive. But as they improve they may give each other support and help in recognizing various ways of facing life in a more honest and independent way. If circumstances are right, group therapy may be useful.

With progressive decline and severe emaciation, hospital admission becomes absolutely necessary as a lifesaving measure. The acute danger to life may not come only from the severe emaciation but also from the serious disturbances in the electrolyte balance, in particular in patients who use vomiting, laxatives, and diuretics to keep their weight at the lowest level. They will continue with such methods even after they have become painfully aware of the dire consequences. In chronic conditions, heroic measures of correcting the electrolyte balance through intravenous infusion are often necessary.

An example of life-threatening acute loss of electrolytes is Yvonne, who had come for treatment at age eighteen and who lived in the dormitory of a college. She had been sick for three years and blamed continuous fighting with her mother, who insisted on supervising her, as having kept her from eating. She promised that she was going to eat since she was now under her own direction. She was sure she could do it alone, that she would eat the proper amounts.

It turned out that she did—but with a dramatic and nearly fatal outcome. She became panicky when she had gained five pounds after two weeks and took laxatives and diuretics by the handful, with the result that she became severely dehydrated and nearly collapsed. She was admitted as an emergency to the hospital, her weight having dropped to sixty-five pounds, with a poor circulatory condition, and her electrolyte level was found to be low. She was given intravenous solutions of electes and glucose; then she received normal hospital food. Her internist advised her to stay in the hospital until her weight was safely above eighty pounds. To this she reacted with enormous anxiety and angry protest, "Do you want me to hate myself?" Until then her attitude toward psychiatric treatment had been somewhat condescending—she did not really need it—but she agreed to cooperate. The experience of intense self-hatred was like an entrance into a more meaningful attitude toward treatment. Even she could see that a person who hates herself for gaining a few pounds must be very unsure and have a low opinion of herself.

Frightening experiences of this type have convinced me that the weight of a patient must be above the danger level for treatment to be carried on outside a hospital. Otherwise the psychotherapist's unease and anxiety will interfere with his therapeutic effectiveness, and the patient's continuous rigid preoccupation with food, characteristic of the starvation state, will make exploration of the relevant dynamic factors virtually impossible. Furthermore, during this extreme state of starvation, anorexics live in such social isolation that the interpersonal experiences explored in psychotherapy are completely absent.

As to the weight to be aimed for, it looks as if there is a certain critical level of weight below which the toxic influence of malnutrition maintains an abnormal mental state. The exact figure for this critical weight is, of course, related to the height and body build of a patient. It is usually around ninety to ninety-five pounds. Though this weight is still far below the normal weight, it is compatible with more normal psychological functioning and the exploration of important and relevant problems can begin. In my consultation work I have seen many patients who had been in ambulatory treatment, usually psychoanalytic in orientation, for as long as five or six years, while their weight had been permitted to remain as low as sixty pounds. Usually the problems within the family had also remained unexplored. Though in treatment, such patients had slipped into the sad state of chronic anorexia.

In my view, the essential weight program should be handled by an internist or pediatrician who has a good and open working relationship with a psychiatrist. This is desirable for many reasons; one important factor is that otherwise patients will play one against the other, a method they have always used at home in pitting father and mother against each other. Mutual understanding and good interaction with the nursing staff and nutritionists are also imperative. Establishing a setting in which the refeeding can take place is more important that the details of what to feed. Treatment at home is possible only when the anxiety level of the parents is not too high, and when they are also in treatment, be it individually, as a couple, or in family therapy. With severe weight loss I prefer weight correction on a medical or pediatric service.

Many anorexics develop enormous anxiety about eating solid food; they will spend hours in eating the smallest amounts, or flatly refuse to eat at all. It is often helpful to prescribe some nutritional preparation, rich in protein and calories, that can be taken in fluid form, and can provide as much as fourteen to eighteen hundred calories daily as basic intake. Such a nutritional supplement should be offered with the explanation that it takes away the anguish of decision-making about when, what, or how much to eat; that instead of having to make choices the patient can drink the prescribed amount in frequent small doses. These nutrients are equally useful for hospital or ambulatory treatment. Tasty and varied ordinary food should be offered in addition. Having to choose a complete meal themselves is too distressing a task for anorexics. They may spend hours on choosing it and will come up with very inadequate meals. To select a meal for them, with due consideration for personal likes and dislikes, is more effective. They all claim that they have to "learn" again what and how much to eat.

Formerly when a patient steadfastly refused to eat, the only way out was tube feeding, which was always considered a distressing method but often the only way of saving a patient's life. In their self-punishing attitude, many anorexics accept tube feeding, some even demand it, because in this way they receive nourishment without having to feel guilty. To others it is reassuring because it makes them feel that the staff and the physician really care for them to go to the trouble of feeding them.

A new way of offering nourishment to a patient unable to take food by mouth, or to the anorexic refusing to do so, has been developed for the postoperative care of surgical patients: intravenous hyperalimentation. Under certain circumstances it is not only helpful in the treatment of anorexia nervosa, but definitely lifesaving. It avoids all the arguments about taking food by mouth and establishes definitely that improvement of the poor nutritional state is a strictly medical problem. It does do away with the deceitful disposing of food, vomiting, and other tricks, though inventive anorexics find ways of interfering with the flow of the fluid, or they turn the whole machinery off. But by bringing about a rather rapid correction of the poor nutrition, it makes patients more accessible to psychotherapy. Solid food should be offered simultaneously and should gradually replace the intravenous alimentation. Before discharge, the patient, now in a greatly improved nutritional state, should be able to maintain her weight on a freely chosen diet.

In deciding on a method of refeeding, the total situation needs to be evaluated. In the following example intravenous feeding was chosen because of the time factor. Zandra had been seen during an extended consultation the previous year; while hospitalized she had gained some weight, but very slowly, only seventeen pounds in two months. She had responded well to a psychotherapeutic trial and decided to come for treatment after she finished college. However, her weight had fallen to below eighty pounds. It had been observed earlier that the severe malnutrition made her unusually rigid and overcontrolled and interfered with therapy. She accepted the need for nutritional improvement and agreed to hospitalization for intravenous feeding. She supplemented the intravenous feeding by eating regular food, more than she had done before. She gained twenty pounds in little more than two weeks without complaining or becoming depressed, and appeared much more relaxed and communicative. She admitted that she felt stronger and more alert, and also enjoyed her prettier appearance.

As her weight increased, she found it easier to eat regular food; it provoked less conflict, whereas during the previous refeeding period every bite had been a major guilt-arousing decision. She began to talk more openly about her contradictory attitude toward her weight and eating, how strongly she had felt for doing as much as, or more than, others in spite of being so thin. For a while it looked as if she might let go of her old inhibitions, and she maintained her weight for a few weeks after discharge. Then there was again a slow decrease. A year later her weight was down to ninety pounds. However, it was possible to do constructive psychotherapeutic work during this period, and she gradually developed a more realistic attitude toward her body and her physiological needs.

Though she had always spoken in very cooperative terms, Zandra had lived with the conviction that what the grown-ups, or people in authority, said did not really matter; she knew that, for her, things were different. This applied in particular to eating and gaining weight. Then she gained two and a half pounds during a relaxed week when she had enjoyed food and had eaten according to her needs. She spoke for the first time openly about her attitude, how she had felt secure in her anorexic state, how she had been convinced that her body would not accept extra food since she objected inwardly to being fat. She had taken a perverse pride in being different, in being able to do without, but had not talked about these secret pleasures because that would have been boastful. She was embarrassed to admit that she took pride in anything, like the fundamentalist who is in danger of no longer being humble when he takes pride in being humble.

The intravenous feeding had interrupted a regressive cycle; progress would have been much slower without the improvement in weight. It took more than a year for Zandra to reach the state of being more permissive, in her term "sloppy," in relation to herself, a relatively short time after nearly six years of anorexic illness.

In recent years overenthusiastic claims have been made for a new method of achieving weight increase, propagated as a complete treatment for anorexia nervosa. It is called behavior modification and rests on the assumption that the food refusal is a learned response that needs to be changed. This is achieved through a reward or punishment system. Weight gain is rewarded, or "positively reinforced," by access to desirable activities, and failure to gain is discouraged by making things unpleasant. In Willa's case three tube feedings a day were used when she failed to gain weight. It is common practice now to put a newly admitted patient to bed in a single room without access to telephone, television, or to other patients or members of the family. A point system is established wherein each "contracted" unit of weight gain gets a certain reward in the form of access to desirable activities. If conditions are disagreeable enough, a patient will do anything to get out of the hospital.

Proponents of behavior modification proclaim its superiority because it achieves weight gain more rapidly than other methods; in a way, it is fool-proof. This claim is probably correct. It also tells why this method so often provokes serious psychological damage. Its very efficiency increases the inner turmoil and sense of helplessness in these youngsters, who feel tricked into relinquishing the last vestiges of control over their bodies and their lives. I have seen a whole series of patients who were discharged as "improved," though they had become depressed, even suicidal, and had developed compulsive binge eating and vomiting. A certain percentage of anorexic patients have always engaged in eating sprees followed by vomiting. This seems to occur much more regularly in those exposed to a coercive method. Once binge eating and vomiting are used as a method for weight control, they have a tendency to become autonomous symptoms that are difficult to change.

As time goes on, most patients become very ashamed
but find it exceedingly difficult to let go of the cycle and
to establish regular control over their eating.

The enthusiasm for behavior modification is not
quite so great as it was a few years ago. Follow-up observations have shown that the weight gain is often
short-lived. Services that use this method have become
selective and will accept only patients who come "voluntarily" and who make a "contract" to gain weight.
Others will make arrangements for work with the families and for psychotherapy for patients. The startling
aspect of such reports is the minute detail with which
the behavior technique is described whereas family therapy and psychotherapy are only briefly mentioned as
something to be carried out by auxiliary personnel. The
more drastic approaches, such as tube feeding as punishment for not gaining weight, seem to be on the way out.

Treatment results are often closely related to the
duration of the illness. In young patients with cooperative parents, soon after the onset of the illness, restitution to normal weight and seemingly adequate social
functioning can be achieved in a relatively short time.
If adequate facilities are available, hospitalization to
restore the weight will cut down the length of treatment, and make constructive work with the family and
patient easier. Even in fresh and mild cases, these various factors need to be integrated. It is easy enough to
produce a short-term weight increase, but this is not
sufficient as treatment and may even be damaging. Not
paying attention to the low weight, as is sometimes done
in psychoanalytic treatment, permitting a patient to
exist at a starvation level, is equally harmful and results
in a chronic anorexic state.

The worst possible fate to anorexics, the reason they all object so vigorously against gaining weight, is losing control over their eating, "blowing up like a blimp." Anything heavier than the emaciated body with which they come for treatment means "fat" to them. If left without therapeutic help, many will become depressed, preoccupied with shame and guilt, if there is a real increase in weight. This is what happened to Alice, whose weight over three years had fluctuated between eighty and one hundred pounds, very low in view of her height of five feet nine inches. At first she had been hospitalized for a behavior modification program; she felt this had been the worst possible regimen for her because nobody paid attention to what she ate as long as she gained weight. She got into the habit of stuffing herself with sweets and candy bars at the end of the day after having eaten no sensible food at all. After discharge she maintained her weight at around ninety-five pounds, considering one hundred pounds as being fat. She came for treatment when she enrolled in college. From the beginning there were difficulties. Her parents not only accompanied her to school but stayed for a week, and she felt reduced to the status of a small child. Her roommate was completely disinterested in her studies but totally preoccupied with a boyfriend. Alice felt excluded, almost displaced from her own room. She made an effort to follow a reasonable diet, even consulted a nutritionist. Within a few weeks it became apparent that things were not going well. She resumed binge eating, as she had during the earlier hospitalization. At first the weight gain appeared desirable and she received many compliments about how much better she looked. She spent the mid-term break with her family and was admired for looking so well, weighing one hundred twelve pounds. After her return she suddenly felt completely unable to handle the situation with her roommate and her eating went wild, with a continuous running to grocery stores and delicatessens, eating constantly day and night. Within one month her weight increased to one hundred forty pounds; she looked well-proportioned but her face showed the rapid increase. She felt unable to concentrate on her studies, became depressed and absorbed by dark suicidal thoughts. She was most alarmed about the way this sudden weight gain had been achieved, by eating junk food only. She had literal images of how all this food would go into her tissues and make them flabby, convincing her that the fat she was carrying around was "shameful fat."

She admitted herself to a psychiatric service to establish control over her eating and for protection against her suicidal impulses. Her weight stabilized within two weeks. Now, a year later, she is a beautiful tall woman, satisfied with her appearance, to whom the idea of going on a starvation regime is completely alien. The reaction of several other anorexic patients who knew her was of particular interest. At first they felt frightened at seeing somebody's weight going out of control. Yet within a short time they noticed that Alice was not only much better-looking, but also much more serene and composed. Without going through such a hectic phase themselves, they felt encouraged to permit their own weight to rise to a normal level.

7

FAMILY
DISENGAGEMENT

The development of anorexia nervosa is so closely related to abnormal patterns of family interaction that successful treatment must always involve resolution of the underlying family problems, which may not be identifiable as open conflicts; on the contrary, quite ofen excessive closeness and overintense involvements lie at the roots. There is no rule on how to handle this, except for one generalization: clarification of the underlying family problems is a necessary part of treatment. Parents tend to present their family life as more harmonious than it actually is, or they deny difficulties altogether. All anorexics are involved with their families in such a way that they have failed to achieve a sense of independence. How to integrate work with the family into other aspects of treatment depends very much on individual circumstances. It is more easily arranged and more commonly accepted when the sick girl still lives at home, or at least in her family's community, even though visits to the therapist may involve traveling many miles.

Bernice, who grew up on a Western ranch, had

been considered happy and healthy until her fourteenth year; she was well built and had started to menstruate early. After some teasing about being chubby, when her weight was one hundred twenty pounds, she suddenly decided she was too large. She also felt that her school-mates didn't like her anymore, that they felt her family was stuck-up. The ranch was successful and was well-known for its breeding stock. Bernice began to stay away from teenage activities, with the explanation that she lived too far away from town, and she also went on a diet, ate less and less, and her weight fell from one hundred twenty to eighty-five pounds within four or five months. Her menses stopped soon after she began her reducing regime. She did not follow the dietary or medi-cal prescriptions of her local physician and a specialist in the larger town. She looked severely emaciated, her weight down to seventy-two pounds, and she was listless and depressed when I saw her in consultation about ten months after the onset of her illness. She had kept very active in spite of her weakness.

During several family sessions the focus was on the question, "What makes it necessary for Bernice to go to the extreme of self-starvation to get attention?" As a child she had been "father's helper," but now her place in the family had become undefined and she had regressed to a clinging relationship with her mother. The mother, too, had felt herself diminished in value since an active grandmother still held the reins on the ranch. It was possible to give some simple recommen-dations: father should report to his wife first and also do things with Bernice, such as going somewhere to-gether at least one evening every other week. Supple-mental nutrition was prescribed in addition to regular meals. I also mentioned that hospitalization would become necessary if there were no appreciable weight gain in the immediate future.

Five weeks later Bernice had gained weight and spoke optimistically about wanting to weigh one hundred pounds before the next visit. The situation seemed generally improved—she had enjoyed the evenings with her father and they felt much more comfortable with each other. But then Bernice became alarmed about gaining too much, and she had lost some weight at the time of the next visit. By then, however, school had resumed and she claimed she felt accepted again by her classmates. When hospitalization was proposed, Bernice pleaded not to miss school; she would eat as much as was needed. This she did and at the next visit, four weeks later, her weight had risen to ninety-nine pounds. She was in excellent spirits and had enjoyed a large party that her family had given for her classmates. Her father described Bernice's new relationship with her peers with an interesting comment: "They are all so happy that she is back with them, and they have welcomed her back." By Christmas Bernice seemed back to normal and she has kept her weight at a desirable level. She maintains the open relationship with her father, is less dependent on her mother, and enjoys her school and has many friends.

This family was open-minded and undefensive in their approach to the illness. Bernice's parents readily agreed, "Of course, we have our problems," spoke about them, and were willing to test out alternatives. Bernice regained a respected place in the family, was able to let go of the anorexia in a rather short time, and joined the activities of her peers.

Celia's father was an executive with an international firm and the family had lived in various foreign countries. Celia was rather upset and resentful about losing her friends after the family returned to the United States when she was sixteen years old. She also took it as a personal affront that one of her grandmothers had a problem with alcohol; the food refusal began during one of grandmother's visits. Celia was at that time a well-developed girl who had been menstruating for several years and who weighed one hundred ten pounds. She was so upset about the grandmother's drinking that she threatened a hunger strike. "If you drink, I don't eat." Grandmother's alcoholism was not cured, but Celia was happy when she became visibly thinner. She continued to lose weight over the next year, with the parents becoming increasingly alarmed and doing everything to make her eat. Finally Celia would take only baby food and demanded spoon feeding, sitting in either father's or mother's lap, forcing her parents to do everything exactly her way. She became completely dependent on her mother, asking to be told everything, whether to go to the bathroom and when to go to bed, crying when she was not told enough. She stopped menstruating and her weight dropped to the low seventies within a year. The condition was diagnosed as anorexia nervosa and she was referred for treatment.

Celia was in very poor condition, pale, shy, and tearful, but accepted staying on the medical service. She lost weight when the choice of food was left to her, and she was put on intravenous feeding. The proportion of intravenous nourishment and food by mouth gradually changed; six weeks later her weight had risen to ninety-eight pounds, and before discharge she maintained it for several days by eating solid foods on her own.

At first she was so evasive and talked in such a low voice that almost no information was obtained. She barely whispered more than "I don't know" or "Nothing troubles me," or she would whine because she felt so guilty. As her nutrition improved, she became somewhat more communicative and then spoke openly about her childhood. She had lived in constant dread of not doing well enough in the eyes of her father, who expected her to be excellent in her academic and athletic performance and also a social success. We gave her an explanation that every person has the right to stand up for herself, that it looked as if the way things had been going had interfered with her becoming the kind of person she was capable of being.

During her hospitalization her parents and brother came three times for evaluation of the family interaction. The mother had read about anorexia nervosa and was rather indignant that there was talk about family problems and underlying dissatisfaction in the marital relationship. She felt that there had never been any dissatisfaction in the marriage, and that the grandmother's drinking was the only upsetting event they had ever experienced. She added that there was something in her husband's manner that caused some people, "probably the supersensitive type," to think that he wasn't pleased with them. The mother behaved in an exceedingly childish way in relation to her husband. He confirmed that in his eyes this had been a great problem, that she was openly subservient to him and continuously asking for reassurance. In the family sessions Celia was at first terribly withdrawn but then, with encouragement and prompting, began to express herself in a more self-assertive way. She finally stated openly that she had always been afraid of criticism and had not felt sure of her parents' love; therefore she could not act like a teenager. She had been isolated from her age group during the past year because formerly her parents had criticized her boyfriend and the group she had been involved with. During the last family session there was an open exchange between Celia and her father, with expressed readiness on his part to acknowledge her right to live her life in her own style, not so gregarious and outgoing as he had wanted. She admitted that she did not need to be so fearful and submissive as she was in the past. It was recognized that she had taken up her mother's problems as her own, so intertwined had they been, instead of pursuing her own life.

Celia made also good use of her individual therapy sessions, where she was told that it was not "bad" to contradict her father or to expect her mother to act more like a grown-up person. She was encouraged to acknowledge that she had wishes of her own and needed help in formulating these wishes. She needed to learn that being kind to herself, indulging herself by being lazy, or doing something just for the fun of it were not bad things but were part of normal growing up, and that she did not need to apologize for them.

The mother remained exceedingly reserved and took little part in the discussion, expressing only the wish that things would go back to the way they used to be. The parents were advised to seek help to resolve the problems in their own relationship; they needed to interact on an adult level so that there was room for the children to grow into more independent people. The younger brother was an active participant, and he took it upon himself to help his sister make social contacts in the new community, where he felt very comfortable. Celia kept in touch by letter, spoke of new friends and mischievous behavior and fights. She seemed to have no trouble with eating; six months later her weight was one hundred five pounds.

Evaluating the development in retrospect, one might say that grandmother's drinking was a blessing in disguise. It gave to this shy and intimidated girl the opening for protesting and for revealing that not everything was as perfect as her meek and helpless mother tried to present it.

Anorexic families vary in their ability and readiness to face the basic problems. Celia's mother tried to cling to a childish dream of perfection, but her husband was more realistic in his appraisal of the situation and insisted on making changes so that the daughter could move out of the confining entanglement with her mother. In Dale's case the mother dominated the home with her denial of any difficulties and a strident demand for perfection. When the facade finally cracked and the real problems came to the surface, she reacted with depression.

The Kaplan family traveled halfway across the country, from Maine to Texas, for a consultation but had little to contribute, except that there was absolutely nothing wrong and that they were at a loss to explain the illness. As in every consultation I had asked all family members for a letter about what each felt had caused the illness. The father and the two daughters (Dale, the older, aged sixteen, was anorexic) wrote an ordinary letter of about a page. The mother sent a typed report of seven single-spaced pages, giving the most minute clinical details, stating over and over that there were simply no emotional problems. The younger sister had expressed openly enough that not everything was well: "It would just burn me up to see her hide her food, feed it to our cat secretly, and then not be strong enough to get on the bus in the morning. I would say to myself 'Why does she have to do this to our family?' " She became upset when a schoolmate asked "When is your sister going to die?" and since then had tried to help and understand Dale—"but it's hard."

Interviewing this family was an exercise in frustration. Whatever question was raised or whatever lead was followed, the answer was "I don't know" or a statement on the order of "You tell us." They had been told they were going to the best authority, and now they expected to be told what was wrong and what to do next. Whether the question concerned past childcare practices, earlier problems, or present anxieties, if there was an answer at all it was immediately modified with "But isn't this natural?" or "Isn't this what normal people do?" There was a vociferous emphasis on their congeniality, how everything had been fine before the illness, never any worries, and how they were all cooperating in helping Dale with this dreadful anorexia. Any effort to help them focus on what really had been going on was smoothly brushed aside. "We just can't figure it out—there is nothing that has troubled us."

When attention was drawn to the fact that Dale had lost over thirty-five pounds before that was noticed, the mother, a school nurse, said, "It was so subtle— even her friends didn't notice anything." This type of not answering directly but quoting someone else to describe the situation is characteristic of anorexic families. The mother also insisted that Dale, whose weight was below seventy pounds at the time, ate more than

her sister. "You'd be surprised at how much she eats—
she eats more than you think." The mother was the
spokesman for the family, and the others agreed with
anything she said. There was a tiny opening when I asked
whether Dale had ever done anything naughty. They
could recall only one incident, that at one time Dale
had not shown a slip from school to her parents but
had signed it herself. This was taken up as something
intimidating in the atmosphere of the home, with a
little girl not daring let it be known that she was in
trouble at school. But it was a dry run: no other episode
was remembered. Whatever topic was touched on, it
was presented in a sentimentalized way. They used
almost identical expressions in talking about themselves
or each other—they all had meant well and everybody
did the best they could. There was little spontaneous
display of feelings. So I gave a number of simple instructions with the intent of unsettling the overrigid
patterns of interaction. One task was that each one
could speak only in his or her own name, that nobody
could explain what somebody else meant. Little if anything of this was put into effect, since nothing was
wrong and nothing needed to change.

On return they were full of complaints that they
had not been properly listened to, that they had not
succeeded in convincing me that the illness had nothing
to do with family problems, that everything was right
with them. About a month or two later, Dale finally
spoke up and stated clearly and definitely, to the shock
and surprise of everybody, that everything was not right,
that they had been hiding problems, and she spoke
openly about things that had been treated as taboo. The
mother became depressed and then was able to express
her angry feelings about "what Dale has done to us."

Briefly stated, what Dale had done was to make apparent conflicts in the marriage which the mother had been totally unable to acknowledge. Now she was alarmed that the marriage might break up. She also spoke with much self-accusation that they had done things which she now felt had been wrong.

The result was that both girls became visibly more independent. Dale began to gain weight, and after she graduated highschool she was able to carry out plans for her own career. The parents stayed together and were able to work out their problems on an adult level, no longer using denial or creating the impression of super-perfection. It is not uncommon for parents to develop symptoms of depression, or for marriage problems to come into the open, when the anorexic child improves and moves away, physically or psychologically, from the confining atmosphere of the home.

These three girls were still living with their families at the time of treatment. On the whole, the younger anorexics are easier to treat than the older ones. But work with the family is just as important in older patients, those in their late teens or early twenties who live away from home, though parents vary even more in their readiness to cooperate. Denial of illness, intrinsic to the anorexic illness, is also characteristic of the families, whose efforts to deny difficulties may go to the extreme—"the anorexia" is blamed as the cause of all current problems. There is a tendency in anorexic families for each member to speak not for him- or herself but in the name of another member, always modifying, correcting, or invalidating what the other person has said. They function as if they could read each other's mind, explaining what the other truly meant. Such features are of various intensity in different families, but add up to a complete denial of illness or of anything in need of change.

Families of young and fresh patients get more readily involved in treatment than those of older girls. After the illness has existed for some time, when the acute anxiety and frenzy about its dangers have subsided, parents are apt to consider the illness a shameful nuisance for which they blame the patient. Although unhappy about the situation, many parents absolutely refuse to be "blamed," a word they use to interpret recommendations for treatment for themselves. If the family problems are not attended to, and parents are motivated by anger and anxiety in their dealings with the anorexic patient, increasingly turbulent situations will develop with frantic mutual accusations. It is of course no easy situation: the anorexic girl can control the whole household with her petulant demands, refusal to eat or threats of suicide, and nothing is done to help her achieve inner security or true independence.

It is not sufficient to advise the parents to show no interest in the youngster's eating or, the opposite, to instruct them to control her eating. It is important that the underlying patterns of interactions are recognized and that the family accept help in changing them. Family therapy has acquired in recent years a certain status of independence as a distinct treatment technique. Enthusiastic reports have come from child-guidance clinics that recommend joint family therapy as the treatment of choice. In my experience this approach is successful in fairly young patients who are relatively healthy emotionally. In those with severe deficiencies in personality development, family therapy is an important and necessary adjunct—but the chief work needs to be done through individual psychotherapy.

Family Disengagement

When parents are well informed and not too defensive, they will make treatment arrangements on their own decision. Edith's mother had become depressed when the anorexia developed; she recognized quite early that the depression was less related to Edith's illness than to her own unacknowledged marital problems. She sought treatment for herself, and her therapist was of great help in encouraging her to be less clinging to her daughter; he arranged for treatment for Edith, who found it difficult to accept that mother no longer was as possessive as she had been in the past. Edith began treatment with the feeling that she had deserted her family, that she had been like a parent in her home, that without her presence the conflicts would come into the open and the family would collapse. When she recognized during a vacation, a year later, the greater independence in her mother, she became more childish and demanding again, complaining that "they" had reduced her to the level of a small child. In reality she resented losing the status she had enjoyed previously by having been the indispensable go-between in her parents' marriage. It is doubtful that these problems could have been clarified so quickly without the mother's going into treatment.

There are families who flatly refuse to become involved in treatment. Some are concerned that bringing problems into the open might be more disturbing than helpful. In one such situation the father stated openly that changing his style of life might reactivate problems that he felt he had handled successfully. In addition, treatment facilities in their home community were inadequate. The anorexic daughter was sent for long-term treatment to a therapeutic hospital noted for the treatment of anorexia. In spite of himself, the father became gradually involved in reevaluating the family patterns. Treatment of this girl was successful, though her parents were not happy that she decided to stay on the Eastern seaboard instead of returning to their Midwestern home.

In another family, difficulties during visits home were used for clarification of underlying factors, through honest examination with the patient and parent. Flora's mother, who lived in a community without adequate psychiatric facilities, came repeatedly for discussion of her problems. During Flora's visits home, she would keep notes on things that disturbed her, restraining her concern or annoyance while the girl was there. As Flora improved and felt more secure in her conviction that therapy was truly to her benefit, not something arranged for by her mother, common conferences became possible during which the disturbances and upsetting scenes were examined. As treatment came to an end, mother and daughter had formed an unusually open, mutually respectful friendship, with much warmth and recognition of their needs and without intrusions on each other. This would not have been possible without the ongoing exploration of the many difficulties that arose during the active phase of the illness.

Parents may also reject treatment for themselves because admitting such a need would imply that their way of raising the child had not been perfect. Usually these are families with serious emotional problems, dominated by the motto, "Spare Mother." Gilda's parents spoke with bitterness about family conferences during earlier treatment efforts, in which they had lashed out at each other with rage and felt that nothing had been learned or accomplished. During the consultation a few points were clarified, in particular that mother had nearly uncontrollable anger about the illness be-

cause she thought Gilda had exposed her to their friends
as an incompetent parent. The father maintained the
basic philosophy of the home, that mother's needs came
first and that what Gilda needed was acceptable only
when it did not infringe on mother's demands. Work
with Gilda was exceedingly difficult; she suffered from
serious emotional disturbances and every visit home
meant a relapse. She felt like a strange specimen, being
inspected for defects and deviations. There were endless
discussions of whether the changes that occurred during
treatment were in agreement with the parents' expectations, or were undesirable and created problems for
them. Gilda felt that the one reason for which her parents had valued her had been her brilliant academic
performance. When she gradually relaxed, they re-
proached her that she was no longer pursuing anything
worthwhile. They were equally critical of her change in
dress style, which became more in keeping with that of
other college girls. Most of their attacks were against
her friends—too selfish, not cultured enough, too superficial. Once when she visited a former friend of whom
they no longer approved, she received a telephone call
that it was urgent to come home, that her father was
sick. The mother felt so strongly about keeping control
over her daughter's life that she pretended this emergency.

There was also continuous and painful debate
about Gilda's eating behavior, her binge eating and
vomiting. When away from home she felt her symptoms
were more or less under control, with one eating binge
at the end of the day. However, at home, every disagreement and criticism provoked an eating binge. This led
to more fighting. If she threw up what she had eaten,
her mother interpreted it as a rejection of herself and

attacked her for it. If she bought food outside the home (charging it to the parents' account), this too was reason for attack. Gilda returned from every visit home like a survivor from a battlefield. She learned only slowly to listen to her parents' complaints and to become considerate of their needs, without relapsing into childlike fighting and renewed weight loss.

These parents had been urgently advised that they needed psychiatric help for their own problems and anxieties, in particular the mother, but they had steadfastly refused the recommendation. Their daughter was "sick, sick, sick" and they wanted her changed back into the girl who had been so pleasing as a child. Gilda knew that therapy had been considered necessary for her parents, and this relieved some of her sense of guilt. She very gradually freed herself, in spite of her parents' frantic efforts not to change, of the rigid growth-impeding patterns that the family had imposed on her. Finally the parents gave up their overdemanding, critical attitude and came to enjoy Gilda's new-found capacity for healthy and more mature living.

8

CHANGING
THE MIND

"I want someone who says 'gaining weight won't make it all right'—I want help with my depression—but nobody listens."

"He would say, 'eat!' as if putting on ten pounds is going to solve all my problems. It's not; solving the problems is going to make me eat."

"They made me put on weight—but did nothing to change my mind."

These are just a few statements in which anorexic patients have expressed their disappointment with treatment efforts that failed them. Such treatment may have focused on making them eat, as is done in the behavior modification approach, or on organic methods such as electroshock treatment or psychotropic medication, or on psychotherapy that never got to important underlying issues. There are few conditions where treatment results are so closely linked to the pertinence of the therapeutic approach. The question is what went wrong in the failed treatment efforts, or what was overlooked.

My concepts of the treatment needs of anorexics have been influenced by seeing in consultation many patients who had not improved, or were getting worse, even though in treatment. The consultant's task is a complex one. He must evaluate the integration of the psychological approach with medical and nutritional management, the combination of individual therapy with the resolution of family problems, and the quality of the patient-therapist interaction. He must also be able to deduce from the data at hand the theoretical assumptions and treatment philosophy of the previous therapist. Furthermore, the readiness of a patient and family to respond to a comprehensive evaluation and to a different treatment approach needs to be assessed.

What has been overlooked before, or what has miscarried, varies of course from case to case. I should like to discuss here only a few recurrent problems. One important source of error is that frequently the focus has been on some isolated facet. Quite often correction of the weight was the main effort while the deeper problems were left untouched. Conversely, some psychotherapists express a wait-and-see attitude concerning the weight, in the unrealistic expectation that the nutrition will improve once the psychological problems have been solved. Such optimism is not only time-consuming; it may be harmful, even fatal. One cannot do meaningful therapeutic work with a patient who is starving. I inform patients who come for consultation that I am not able to give a meaningful opinion on their psychological condition until a certain degree of nutritional restitution has taken place. Although always advocating the need for an integrated treatment approach, I shall focus here on the problems of the psychotherapeutic process itself.

It seems that many therapists in approaching an anorexic patient are tied to outmoded concepts of psychoanalytic treatment, even those who otherwise work with contemporary concepts. Many stress the symbolic meaning of the noneating and the underlying unconscious problems, fantasies, and dreams, and interpret their unconscious meaning to the patient. When the traditional psychoanalytic setting is examined in transactional terms, one can recognize that for these patients it may signify the reenactment of some damaging experience in their past. Anorexics grow up in harmonious-looking, well-meaning families where they are often the most valued child, one who at the same time had been most rigidly controlled. They have felt obliged to fulfill the great expectations of others and failed to develop true autonomy and initiative. They experience "interpretations" as indicating that someone else knows what they truly mean and feel, that they themselves do not understand their own thoughts. The goal of individual therapy should be to help them develop a valid self-concept and the capacity for self-directed action. The therapist's task is to assist patients in uncovering their own abilities and resources for thinking, judging, and feeling. "Giving interpretations" contradicts this goal. It does not matter whether or not an interpretation is correct; what is harmful is that it confirms a patient's fear of being defective and incompetent, doomed to dependence.

Many who have been in previous treatment complain that what the therapist explained to them did not make sense but that he had tried to force them to agree. Anorexics have a tendency to comply with what is said, but if they feel it stands too much in contrast with what they think, they will object. Irene (Chapter Four) complained that her previous therapist stubbornly insisted that he was always right. She gave as an example a dream about a Red Queen, which he interpreted as meaning that she had been afraid of menstruation and was concerned with being bad. She was very definite that he had been wrong; she remembered how she had felt at the time and knew that she had not been afraid of menstruation.

Irene was a well-developed child who had shown beginning pubertal development at age twelve, when her weight was somewhat above one hundred pounds. She began to control her weight, lost a few pounds, and then maintained her weight at ninety-five pounds; during this time she grew four inches. The signs of pubertal development gradually diminished and she did not menstruate.

She was nearly eighteen years old when she was seen in consultation, and she stressed that she had not been afraid of menstruation, had never given it a thought. As we discussed her life situation in general and her relationship to her classmates' activities, I expressed amazement that, living in such close contact with other adolescent girls, she had not thought about menstruation. She then admitted that she had disliked it when her breasts began to develop and that she was pleased when they nearly disappeared as she grew taller and thinner. Finally she interrupted herself with the question, "Do you think it was more abnormal that I never gave it a thought than if I had been afraid of menstruation?" After that she examined in great detail the concerns and problems of that period: she had been afraid of becoming a teenager and of the new social demands, and the biological act of menstruation had seemed relatively unimportant. For the subsequent exploration it was important to keep encouraging her to discover the meaning and significance of her ideas and behavior, without my interpretation.

Changing the Mind

Most patients who come for consultation have been exposed to a variety of treatment approaches, which often have been inconsistent, and they have developed an endless variety of tricks to defeat them. Therapists in turn try to avoid a head-on collision with the patient's wish not to gain weight, and they will not confront an anorexic with her manipulative and intimidating behavior. Greta, a twenty-two-year-old girl who had been anorexic for over six years, and who had been almost continuously in treatment, reacted with panic to my questions about the development of her difficulties. When during the family session an attempt was made to focus on her role in the family, she refused to participate. Afterwards Greta had a severe hysterical outburst, screaming and shrieking so that her mother demanded hospitalization. My suggestion that we would find out during the next session what was so troublesome had a soothing effect.

During the exploration on the following day this seemingly shy and meek girl was rather aggressive, attacking me as well as the referring physician, shouting "I am here on trial!"—she was being accused of being sick in order to punish her parents, and nobody considered that she was punishing herself more than others. I stated quietly that I could not have possibly spoken of her punishing her parents since she had expressed no opinion at all. Her repeated complaints about her previous therapist had been "Nobody listens." I pointed out that the exact opposite was true, that she refused to participate when she was asked what she might have to say. It had become apparent that, whenever the focus was not entirely on blaming others, she would stop communicating and begin her accusations.

But having it pointed out that her behavior did influence others conveyed to her that she was not as passive and helpless as she tried to present herself. Greta began to talk more openly about what really troubled her, how isolated she felt, how shy she was with people, how easily her feelings were hurt, and how she would withdraw when things did not go her way. She had made isolation a way of life, and her whole behavior was an open message: "Don't touch me! I'm so anxious—I can't be bothered with anything." She summarized it as "pushing the panic button" whenever something didn't go according to her plans, and she admitted that this had interfered with her progress in therapy. As this theme was elaborated, she gradually became actively interested in exploring alternatives to her present way of life. Greta realized that she had to stop using weakness as a weapon and sickness as an embodiment of her power and strength. She had been aware of the seriousness of the underlying problems but had kept this a secret because she did not believe that anybody could understand.

The most common complaint of patients about their previous treatment experience is that they did not know what therapy was about or that they felt that their problems had not been understood. Whether a patient is accepted for long-term treatment or is seen in consultation only, it is important to communicate in the very first session that the illness can be understood and that there is help for it—and this needs to be spelled out in detail. Many who had been in treatment complain that they had found it difficult to talk with their therapist, that there had been long silences, or that he focused on topics they felt did not matter or did not understand. It is important to explain in some detail what the illness is all about. Most are surprised that so much is known about it and that ideas and feelings they consider their own personal secrets have been expressed by others, sometimes in exactly the same words. This preliminary feeling of understanding can be established by detailed relevant questions or in the form of an explaining talk. How to proceed will depend on the patient's ability to communicate. Some are reluctant to speak spontaneously, and then a lengthy explanation is in order. Others want to be sure that what they have to say is listened to and understood; they respond better to questions. If things go well, it is not uncommon for a patient to ask, "Did you have it yourself?"—indicating that she feels that what is discussed is relevant. It is important not to appear omniscient or as if you have mind-reading abilities. I emphasize that what I know I have learned from other anorexic patients. They don't like this because they want to be unique.

I should like to give as an example my first interview with Helen, a seventeen-year-old girl whose therapist had asked for a consultation because he felt no progress was being made; she was reluctant to talk or even admit that she was ill. Helen confirmed that she just sat there silently and resented the fact that money was spent on treatment where the time was not used. I took this as a message that this was one of the situations where I would have to do most of the talking, and I explained that I had learned some general principles from other youngsters with the same condition.

The main thing I've learned is that the worry about dieting, the worry about being skinny or fat, is just a smokescreen. That is not the real illness. The real illness has to do with the way you feel about yourself.

The Golden Cage

There is a peculiar contradiction—everybody thinks you're doing so well and everybody thinks you're great, but your real problem is that you think that you are not good enough. You are afraid of not living up to what you think you are expected to do. You have one great fear, namely that of being ordinary, or average, or common—just not good enough. This peculiar dieting begins with such anxiety. You want to prove that you have control, that you can do it. The peculiar part of it is that it makes you feel good about yourself, makes you feel "I can accomplish something." It makes you feel "I can do something nobody else can do," and then you start to think that you are a little bit better because you can look down on all these people who are sloppy and piggish and don't have the discipline to control themselves. There is only one problem with this feeling of superiority. It doesn't solve your problem because what you really want is to feel good about yourself while feeling happy and healthy. The paradox is that you have started to feel good for being unhealthy.

By this time there had been a change in the way she was looking at me. She came in solemn, dour, downcast, but with a challenging expression of "I dare you to tell me what the matter is." Now the expression was one of questioning: maybe there is something to be learned. She started to give some information about her background, parents, siblings, and experiences in school. The theme, as usual, was that there had never been any problems, that she had been doing well. I took this up:

This is one of the great problems—I've heard the same from many kids and so I assume you have it too. They always did what was expected, but never knew what they themselves wanted. When it came to receiving presents, they were very grateful for what they were given but never felt that what they received was the real thing. Still, they didn't know what to ask for. Some even feared not having a mind of their own, or the right to live their own life, and they have always done what was expected. What is the most daring thing you ever did? [No answer.] I mean something you did because you wanted to do it and not because they expected it or would be pleased with it. Maybe you can't think of anything because you never knew that you have the right to live your own life. This illness is the supreme effort to establish for oneself the conviction that "I can do what I want to do. I can do it the way I want and not the way everybody else does." But it is a very painful way of doing because it means denying your own physical comfort; it means sacrificing the enjoyment of what you really want.

You did it now by losing thirty-five pounds in six months—and you show how much suffering that implies. You must have denied yourself eating when hungry, though actually your thoughts are always about food and how much you would like to eat. Only you don't permit yourself to do it. This is the grave question, why healthy kids deny themselves the enjoyment of life. What I've heard from so many others—I don't know if it applies to you, but I'm pretty sure it does— is that they don't permit themselves to enjoy life because they feel guilty. Guilty for not living up to what they were supposed to be, guilty for having thoughts of doing something entirely different. Even with all the success in school and in other things, there is much anger about having to push yourself and being always worried about not doing well enough. There is also anger and envy about denying yourself the enjoyment of just loafing or doing what you really want to do. So we have this dreadful confusion of forcing yourself to do something, like not eating, that is not what you truly want to do. You feel guilty for doing it, but also you don't know what you yourself want to do. What really bothers you is that you don't even know what to expect of life or what would make you happy. And then this illness comes, and thinking about food overshadows everything.

Now I needed to give an explanation that the terrific preoccupation with food is directly related to the starvation, and will continue as long as food is denied.

You think you are worthwhile only if you do something very special, something so great and dazzling that your parents and other people you care about will be impressed and admire you for being super-special. I don't know your particular dream of glory, but I'm sure you won't be satisfied with anything ordinary. It is this feeling of obligation of having to do something very special that makes your life so hard and dreary and makes you work so compulsively. Some feel starving makes it easier because they feel so pleased with themselves just for being able to do it. For a short time it feels as if all pressure is gone. As a matter of fact, eating anything upsets you because this pride of getting thinner seems a reassurance that everything will be all right.

This led to another area. Helen was in the last year of highschool and though her grades were fairly high, better than ever before, she was dissatisfied: "I think I could do better than I did." I answered:

Changing the Mind

Much unhappiness comes from not having as many friends as you'd like to have, or that the others don't really understand you, and you become kind of lonely and isolated. I hear from many that they feel they are not really part of the group. Maybe they even feel that the others are sloppy, or don't care about important things, or maybe they're uninterested, maybe vulgar. But that is a very lonely place to be, to strive so hard and to do the best, to find yourself superior but all alone.

It is important that the various symptoms are openly discussed, and I said:

Many say that they feel full, they don't need to eat, they have had enough. In reality they are aching to eat more, to be warm, and not to be so bony. They say they enjoy being skinny, but I know from many that it hurts them to sit down, and it is real agony to spend a day in school. Others feel cold all the time but deny that this suffering is going on. One thing you don't know but I can tell you—this suffering is not the way to a solution. It makes you feel special but it doesn't accomplish what you really want and need, and it doesn't prevent your feeling unhappy. You need to feel that you're living your own life, to feel worthwhile and that what you do is truly what you want for yourself. You are entitled to do all this without feeling guilty, whether it's for your ambition or for not doing well in school, and to permit yourself to be a person who enjoys life. Many of the things that truly trouble you are of such an order that you don't even want to admit them to yourself. At this moment you take so much pride in being so skinny that you have sacrificed everything else to it. To get well demands a new, greater sacrifice—namely, giving up this unnatural pride in something that doesn't accomplish anything.

So it was with Helen. Patients who have been sick and in various forms of treatment for many years, and who are rather cynical about the possibility of finding help for their unhappiness, will relax and open up when the focus is put on finding out what they want and expect. This of course is only an opening for the therapy. It does not accomplish more than giving a ray of hope that their problems can be understood and may be resolved. It does not suddenly remove all the misconceptions with which they have conducted their lives and the iron determination with which they pursue goals based on those misconceptions. But once it has been stated clearly that they suffer from inner doubt and uncertainties, not from an appetite disorder, their agreement to this becomes a thread to hang on to through the maze of denial, contradictions, and determination not to change that characterizes the therapeutic involvement in anorexia nervosa.

Nor does a hostile attitude toward psychiatry preclude the establishment of a working relationship. Irma had been hospitalized with a dangerously low weight after a year and a half of anorexic illness. When her physician suggested a psychiatric consultation, she screamed at him, "You're crazy! I won't go to a crazy doctor!" When she came for a consultation, several months later, she attacked her mother: "You dragged me here. I'm not going to say a word." But she began to answer several orienting questions, that the weight loss had occurred when she suddenly dropped out of college. She felt the only reason she had gone to college was to please her parents. She now was working at a job she didn't like, but she didn't know what she wanted to do. Her mother's leaving the room revived Irma's anger. "Please, Mom, don't make me stay here—I'll only get worse" and "I want to get out of here. I hate you, I hate her, I hate everybody—I just want to get out of here!" The question "When did you begin to feel so much hatred and so harassed by everybody?" was answered with a denial: "I don't feel harassed by everybody. I have many friends that I love." When I commented, "From what you say you have met many unfeeling persons in your life. Let's see how this happened," she shouted, "I didn't say that. You're putting words in my mouth!" I said, "Oh, I understood you to say that you hated everybody. I apologize for having drawn the wrong conclusion." Her comment was, "I really don't hate everybody. I didn't mean it the way it sounded."

By now the crying had stopped, and I inquired about the relationship with her parents. "From what I heard you say, and you said it repeatedly, your parents kind of overinfluenced you. You sounded as if your parents were telling you what to do. And the other thing I heard you say was that you felt you never had a chance to set your own goals and find out what you wanted. Talking some more about this might be of some help. Maybe you can discover what you truly want." Irma: "Whenever I said I'm going to quit they would just say, 'All right, don't go on. Quit if you want to' and then they would say, 'but' . . . blah, blah, blah, and give me twenty reasons why I shouldn't quit. I finally did quit last year and so I proved they had been right, that I couldn't do anything." When it was suggested that discussing these things might be of help, she returned to her old attack: "It makes me feel crazy. I've always had the idea that people who go to a psychiatrist are crazy." But she agreed that this fear might be unreasonable, and it would help her with her deep sense of dissatisfaction and unhappiness to understand what was behind it.

Irma appeared relaxed and agreeable during the second interview and talked freely about her background, how she and her older sister had felt forced to study and go to college. The sister had been rebellious and Irma felt it her obligation to make up to her parents where the sister had failed them. She spoke about her mother: "She has controlled my life so long, now I have to control her." Mother had insisted on their going to an out-of-town college, "to make us independent." Irma felt stymied by this, that if she wanted to be independent she would still be doing what mother wants her to do. She used to feel close to her mother but recognized now that something is wrong when a mother keeps her children so close that they have to fight to get free of her. Then she asked me for help with her sleeping, though she knew it was hunger that kept her awake. She became so depressed at night that she went on an eating binge and then became more depressed. "I really have tried all my life not to give them trouble, and now I am so guilty for giving them trouble." She accepted the need for treatment when what we had discussed was summarized as: "There is something you don't even know, that you have a right and duty to live your own life. And this is where therapy can help you. That is what a psychiatrist does, help you to find out what you really want to do with your life."

A successful initial interview does no more than arouse interest in the possibility that therapy may be useful, that there are underlying problems that are understandable and may be accessible to change. It does not do away with the inherent treatment difficulties that are related to the characteristic personality traits and the whole development of these girls. They feel they have found the perfect solution and will cling for a long time to their preoccupation with weight. Even if the serious malnutrition is corrected early in treatment, almost against the patient's will, she will cling to the notion that she must exercise control over her body. The ups and downs in the weight curve often reflect what is going on: rigid clinging to an outdated position, or anxiety about facing issues and problems that had been vigorously denied. Anorexics frequently do not want to talk about their weight or have it referred to, and therapists may submit to this demand. This I consider antitherapeutic. The problems that come up in connection with weight changes offer important material for psychotherapeutic exploration. The important underlying issues will not become truly accessible for therapeutic exploration until the patient has achieved a harmonious attitude toward her body and faces the world as the person she is, not as a tightly controlled organism.

The task of psychotherapy in anorexia is to help a patient in her search for autonomy and self-directed identity by evoking an awareness of impulses, feelings, and needs that originate within her. Therapeutic focus must be on the patient's failure in self-expression, on the defective tools and concepts for organizing and expressing needs, and on the bewilderment in dealing with others. Therapy represents an attempt to repair the conceptual defects and distortions, the deep-seated sense of dissatisfaction and isolation, and the conviction of incompetence.

The therapist's task is to be alert and consistent in recognizing any self-initiated behavior and expression on the part of the patient. To do so he must pay minute attention to the discrepancies in a patient's recall of the past and to the way she misperceives or misinterprets current events, to which she will then respond inappropriately. The therapist must be honest in confirming or correcting what the patient communicates. When held to a detailed examination of the when, where, who, and how, real or fantasied difficulties and emotional stresses will come into focus and the patient will discover the problems hidden behind the facade of her abnormal eating behavior. All of this demands sensitive recognition of what the patient herself contributes: she thus makes the experience that what she expresses is listened to, something she had been deprived of during her early development. Many complain that this had not taken place during previous therapeutic experiences.

The picture of the development of the illness that I have presented in this book is based on what I have learned during psychotherapy with many different patients. Therapy aims at liberating patients from the distorting influences of their early experiences and encouraging them to look at their own development in more factual terms. This is a difficult task because patients will adhere to their distorted concepts, the false reality with which they have lived, since it represents their only way of having experiences and communicating; they will let go of this only slowly and reluctantly. Their whole life is based on certain faulty assumptions that need to be exposed and corrected. Deep down every anorexic is convinced that her basic personality is defective, gross, not good enough, "the scum of the earth," and all her efforts are directed toward hiding the fatal flaw of her basic inadequacy. She is also convinced that the people around her, her family, friends, and the world at large, look at her with disapproving eyes, ready to pounce and to criticize her. The picture of human behavior and interaction that anorexics form in their smooth-functioning homes is one of surprising cynicism and pessimism.

Therapy must help the patient to uncover the error of these convictions, to let her recognize that she has substance and worth of her own, and that she does not need the strained and stressful superstructure of an artificial ultra-perfection. I have stressed the need to confront an anorexic patient with the fact that her behavior arouses anxiety and guilt in others. Helping her to become aware that her behavior and attitude have an effect on people, even a negative one, may be the first step in her discovery that she is not completely ineffective. A precondition for this work is a trusting and dependable relationship, and for this to develop it is important that even slight and seemingly innocent distortions and misrepresentations are recognized and acknowledged. Treatment with anorexics involves the great problem of establishing honest communication. As a group they are manipulative and deceitful; anything goes in their effort to defeat a weight-gaining program. You have to establish from the beginning that psychotherapy deals with their inner self-doubt, not with weight and dieting.

On principle, anorexic patients resist treatment. They feel that in extreme thinness they have found the perfect solution to their problems, that they obtain the respect they had missed all their life. They do not complain about their condition—on the contrary, they glory in it. Yet in spite of this, most are aware that there is something wrong with the way they approach life and that they need help with their unhappiness. Treatment conditions and problems vary from patient to patient. They are most difficult in those who get caught in the binge–vomiting routine. The element of dishonesty is much more severe. Whenever they were confronted with a situation that provoked anxiety, they avoided solving it and instead indulged in an eating binge; they are unwilling to let go of this escape route for the seemingly dubious advantage of leading a more competent life. Eventually they have to face the basic issues. The earlier the deceitful maneuvers are interrupted, the greater the chance of effective resolution of the illness.

A seriously delaying but often overlooked factor is the enormous compliance with which these youngsters can approach treatment, having lived their whole lives in an overconforming way. They agree with everything that is being said, will elaborate on it, even fabricate material that they feel the therapist wants to hear. This is one more reason why an interpretative approach is so ineffective in this condition. Anorexics will agree with what has been said, quote it in a different context, but actually feel that it means nothing.

While dutifully and compliantly agreeing, anorexics cherish the secret knowledge that things as they are being discussed are not so. Throughout childhood they have been double-tracking, agreeing with what is demanded of them but secretly disowning it with the thought of "I know better." Some will explain in detail how their sense of integrity, of individuality, of not being a nothing or "swallowable," depended on this inward knowledge, which of course they would never express openly: *they* (the grown-ups) were wrong. The therapist needs to be aware of this. If things go too smoothly and there is ready agreement with everything being discussed, the question must be raised, "What is she really thinking?" Pseudo-agreeing may manifest itself in every area under discussion—in reviewing their background and homelife, when talking about friends, in explaining their self-concept, or in expressing their attitude toward weight and eating. It applies also to treatment goals, particularly to the question of "growing up" and "maturing." Many will readily agree to this as their goal, that they want to become independent people, even though their total behavior reflects their fear of adulthood and the grim determination not to grow up.

Such an inner contradiction was vividly expressed in Janet's behavior. After three years of anorexic illness she claimed that she was unhappy about her low weight. She was aware that she differed from other anorexics, who said they didn't want to gain, protested against the demand, and would engage in all kinds of deceits to slow down the process. The trouble was that those who protested did gain weight at a reasonable rate, whereas she, in spite of all her agreeable protestations, was terribly slow in gaining during a lengthy hospitalization. Afterwards she lost this weight again, despite repeated statements of how eagerly she wanted to gain. It was only when normal weight became a practical necessity (to enter graduate school) that she admitted how, through all these years of claiming that she wanted to gain weight, she had the inner conviction of "I won't, I won't." She was inwardly so opposed to gaining weight that she had been sure her body would cooperate by not doing it. She admitted: "I know not wanting to mature and have a female body is a child's way of looking at life. I never wanted to grow up—I always felt I should stay a child in my parents' home." She had been a brilliant student but with the belief that she was simply doing what others expected of her, that all these accomplishments were useless as far as she herself went. She permitted her secret reservations to come into the open only after treatment had helped her to recognize that she was capable of leading a life of her own.

Signs of change and progress are often minute and need to be acknowledged by the therapist so that the patient comes to believe in her ability to change. Karen became depressed and anorexic during the last year of highschool, convinced that the others did not like and respect her because she had "a stomach." She accumulated evidence that she had felt insecure since kindergarten—even then the in-group did not accept her because she was not "good enough"—but that she had fought against being one of the nobodies. She went into great detail describing the differences between the "peers" and the "peons" and how your fate in the upper school was determined by the position you had held in lower and middle school. While elaborating later on this topic, there was a slight hesitation and a change in her posture, to which I paid attention. In an entirely different tone of voice she corrected herself, saying that it was not true, that the girls she had envied when younger were neither academically nor socially more successful than the others. This was nothing more than a first crack in her conviction that the size of her figure and the flatness of her stomach determined her status and attractiveness. She responded well to being praised for her honesty in having admitted an error in her thinking, that this was a good sign, that she could learn to correct other errors in the painful and troublesome convictions that dominated her self-concept.

Several weeks later, on meeting another anorexic patient, Karen had a similar corrective insight. "I've just finished talking to an anorexic girl, and in listening to her I realized the deception that takes place in oneself in a case of anorexia nervosa. She said when she was depressed, she *could* not eat and I realized that wasn't true. She made me realize how stupid I am in worrying about my stomach and my weight to the extreme I've been doing." This was of course not the end of her anxiety about her worth, but she would now announce a relapse with a slightly joking remark, "the fog has come back," meaning the contrast to the clarity she felt when not preoccupied with her weight.

Lucy had been unusually rigid in everything she did. During her sessions she would sit up straight, scarcely moving, and recite her activities in a somewhat mechanical way. One day she came in and dropped down on the couch, leaning backwards, visibly relaxing, with a genuine exclamation, "Gosh—it feels good to sit down; it was just one of those days." She elaborated on the many problems that had come up and how she had rushed around all day. This might seem a small thing, but in Lucy's case it was nearly revolutionary that she admitted to weakness and fatigue, feelings of annoyance, and the desire to relax. It was not the end of her being overproper and overpolite. But it was a red-letter day to refer back to, that she could be accepting of her own feelings, not always obliged to exercise constant rigid control and never reveal them.

Such changes take place in many areas. As the self-concept improves and their style of thinking matures, the way patients remember their background and development will also change. As they become more active participants in therapy, they gradually recognize that things did not just happen, but that they themselves had played an active role in their life of seeming submission and exaggerated expectations.

During the height of the illness anorexics are so preoccupied with how they appear in the eyes of others, constantly absorbed in proving their superiority or camouflaging their inferiority, that their style of communication is rather stilted, often pretentious and always dead serious, completely lacking in humor. It is important for the therapist to be simple, down to earth, and unambiguous in his communication. Whenever possible I use colloquial expressions; if something can be said in a lighter vein, so much the better. Anorexics take themselves and their symptoms so seriously that some may react as if they were being attacked with sarcasm (a tone definitely to be avoided). But if the light comment is made in a friendly, well-meaning way, this discrepancy in understanding may lead to an investigation of their own cynical view of the world. Gradually even the most dour anorexic will recognize that every bite she eats is not a world-shaking event, nor is a less than perfect-grade reason for despair. More than with any other patients I use episodes and experiences from my own daily life to illustrate some point. Visits with children are apt to furnish good examples of normal self-assertion or constructive competition, or of a child's way of interpreting experiences in a childish way, something that is often recognizable in an anorexic's thinking. Sometimes an episode from another patient's story (anonymous, of course) may clarify something that this patient has not been able to recognize in herself. When I told Lucy the story of the girl who hated Westminster Abbey because her father would "force" her to go there, she recognized the girl's misperception. Every time the girl's family visited London, her architect father visited the Abbey. The daughter, having been there several times, would have preferred to go shopping with her mother but felt her father would be angry and hurt if she did not go with him; then she would feel guilty for disappointing him. Thus she felt forced to accompany him. Lucy reacted by saying, "The way I felt forced to eat dessert." She had always thought that her father, who had a sweet tooth, and the cook who prepared the dessert would be disappointed if she did not eat it; so she had felt "forced." She had repeatedly presented the story about the dessert as proof of factual coercion, always adding, "At least they couldn't force me to enjoy it." Hearing of a similar reaction in another girl, in an entirely different context, helped to recognize the distortion in her own reaction.

This was the beginning of Lucy's freeing herself from other erroneous convictions. Some time later she spoke about having truly enjoyed listening to a friend play the piano, but that it had made her feel sad at the same time. Though a fairly good musician, she had never liked playing the piano because she had felt forced to take piano lessons. Recognizing the unrealistic aspect of this feeling, she now felt free to enjoy music and decided to take piano lessons again, this time because *she* wanted it.

The pleasant going-along of anorexics serves to a large extent the purpose of avoiding the possibility of any disagreement. Yet psychotherapy is a process during which erroneous assumptions and attitudes are recognized, defined, and challenged so that they can be abandoned. It is important to proceed slowly and to use concrete small events or episodes for illustrating certain false assumptions or illogical deductions. The whole work needs to be done by reexamining actual aspects of living, by using relatively small events as they come up. Most patients will avoid conflict by going along with whatever is discussed. Then a new situation comes up and it becomes apparent to the therapist that what seemed clarified earlier had not been truly integrated.

Mara was a past master in this. Like other anorexics she was troubled by feelings of emptiness, not knowing what role to play, hating herself for gaining weight, but mostly by the question: "Why should anybody like me?" She had been in treatment for over a year, and the possible background of these feelings had been repeatedly discussed; she made reassuring statements on many occasions that she now felt that she was truly herself. A few weeks later something would happen to show how her undoing mechanisms had been quietly at work. She had politely listened to explanations but nullified them inside. She had never shown emotion, never corrected or protested any formulation.

Once on a shopping trip Mara was suddenly tormented by the question, "Who do I want to be?" and she was shocked that she had fallen back into role playing, again preoccupied with the question, "What is me? When I'm alone I can't define what I'm like. I can see qualities but nothing that adds up to being me. I can't see why people like me. My real fear is that I'll let go and that then I'll hate myself." As before she would recite this as a statement of fact, that she had always known this, that she was not worthy.

Again I told her: "Every girl who becomes sick with this illness lives with certain convictions and rules of living that are not only not helpful but downright harmful. Your expression 'I hate myself if I gain weight' is a dramatic example of such an erroneous assumption. There is nothing hateful about you or your body. When I say something like that you seem to agree but you don't truly believe it. In this way we miss the real problem, and you don't explore the background of this false conviction. As long as you are absolutely determined not to argue, you'll cling to your secret convictions. As far as learning or changing anything goes, it's a dead end."

This time she linked her fear of being deceived to the way she had always felt deceived in her family when nobody paid attention when she was miserable. "I felt right along that I was leading a fake life—always in fear of failing." This time she really listened to the explanation of how the continuous anxiety that her real self was not good enough had forced her into this fake existence, always haunted by the question of "Who am I?" I explained to her that this self-devaluation is the essence of the illness—and she could get free of it only if she accepted her genuine self, undeveloped as it might be, as good enough for her.

Following this session Mara gradually relaxed in the excessive demands she made on herself. Until then, only work that demanded extreme effort gave her the feeling of accomplishment; work that she enjoyed or that came easy was not worthwhile. She became more at ease socially and began to enjoy friendships—just so, not to prove something about herself. Her weight gradually rose to a normal level, with some amusement on her part that it did not really matter when she broke through another of her many "ceilings," and with some amazement that she could eat and enjoy food as her weight, after some ups and downs, stabilized at its pre-illness level. Some time later a new anorexic girl, seeing Mara leave the office, asked, "What about the girl with the smiling face? Has she had it too?" Seeing that smile was reassuring to her—there was hope that the deep anguish of the illness could be resolved and she, too, might look forward to enjoying life again.

The anorexic's gaining of trust in her own abilities, and the conviction of her own worth, is a slow process and needs to be explored in many different areas. The conviction of being inadequate and unworthy is so deep-seated and of such long standing that she withdraws behind the mask of superiority whenever she experiences the slightest self-doubt or encounters disagreement. Anorexics, like other patients only more so, are afraid of change and of abandoning the false reality by which they live. Lacking inner guideposts they have relied excessively on the praise and good opinion of those around them. They feel safe from blame and criticism only when they can maintain the image of perfection in the eyes of others. This need dominates their behavior during treatment and confronts the therapist with a double-edged task. He must disagree with their erroneous assumptions and, at the same time, not only support but encourage or elicit the potential for a positive self-image. Patients let go of the negative self-image and the fear of being condemned as insignificant only as they come to trust the therapist's genuine interest in and appreciation of their individual assets and abilities, and his genuine belief that they have a true personality of their own. This requires the therapist to differentiate between the genuine and the facade performance.

If therapy proceeds with consistent focus on the patient's self-doubt, indecisiveness, and self-devaluation, progress will gradually manifest itself in many areas of living—increasing reliance on their own feelings and thinking, greater self-acceptance, and a more harmonious and prideful attitude toward their body and their maturing into adulthood.

An important sign of progress is the development of new friendships. During the acute phase of the illness, anorexics are completely isolated and self-absorbed. With improvement they become more interested in others and long for warm and affectionate relationships. Having been out of contact for so many years, they often need help with the practical aspects of human relationships, and even more to know what one can reasonably expect from a friendship. As children they had been overvalued by their parents, and thus they are apt to feel rejected without continuous praise and positive reinforcement, or when there is any disagreement or criticism. They are slow in developing meaningful heterosexual relationships. In some there is a great desire to be considered attractive, and having many boyfriends serves the function of reassuring them in that respect. Others cling to the conviction that Love will cure them and will make all difficulties disappear—with the result that the young men quickly disappear, to escape this superhuman task. The commitment to marriage is usually postponed until they have tested out their capacity to feel independent and free and have become inwardly secure and self-reliant.

I am in the habit of asking my patients toward the end of treatment how they feel about having had this illness and what role therapy has played. None has expressed regret about having been anorexic. Most feel that without it they might have been stuck with their overdependent attitude toward the family, or might have become mentally sick in other ways. Some feel embarrassment about the mentality behind it, that they could have been so immature and childish in their whole behavior during that time. The very idea that they tried to solve their problems through starving, and by trying to be the kind of person they were not, has now become incomprehensible. Answering the question of whether they would have reached this maturity and new sense of well-being without treatment, they all say they could not have done it on their own. They feel the greatest benefit has been that they understand themselves and others better, that they have gained a different view of their parents and their relationship to them. In particular they understand other young people better, and this they consider a benefit for life.

When Naomi was asked how she would have done without treatment, she answered without hesitation, "I think I probably would never have gone beyond eighty-five pounds or so and would have been continuously hysterical about the scale. I probably would have become a very unrelaxed person, good in my career but constantly worried about not being good enough. I think that worry about being special, about being really outstanding and pleasing my family, would have persisted. I didn't feel that I had the right to be anything but outstanding, that it was almost in my genes because I thought everybody in my family was brilliant. I went through life scared stiff that I would be a flop and would never prove to them that I was a worthwhile person." In her treatment the term "being good enough" had been examined in many ways. Initially she had no concept or feeling of what would be enough. "Enough means when you collapse, when your body just won't give up any more of itself." Gradually she recognized, "You give

what you have to give and not what you don't have."
Now that she has recovered from the illness, she feels
she has a message for others: "Tell people and make
them understand there is no merit in starving. It just is
not true that you are superior by going hungry."

Therapeutic work with these girls is admittedly difficult, slow, and at times exasperating. In a way they
have to build up a new genuine personality after all the
years of fake existence. There is nothing more reward-
ing than seeing these narrow, rigid, isolated creatures
change into warm, spontaneous human beings with a
wide range of interests and an active participation in
life. During the illness they looked and behaved as if
they were constructed from the same erector set, mouth-
ing the same stereotyped phrases from the same broken
record. It is truly exciting to see the emergence of highly
individualistic personalities after these years of sterile
self-absorption.

In conclusion I should like to illustrate how the
change in image reflects the change from feeling like a
helpless victim of circumstances to the experience of
being an active participant in life. During the first year
of treatment Ida, whom you met in Chapter Two, used
the image of a sparrow in a golden cage to describe her
position in her family. She felt she was not made for the
luxury and elegance of her home; she did not want to
be on display and longed to be inconspicuous, free to
move around and express her own ideas. When I asked
her about this image toward the end of treatment, she
remembered it but thought she would explain it differently now. The idea of having been caged in was still
with her, but she felt that she herself had created the
cage. "Once you set a pattern for yourself, you want to

The Golden Cage

live up to what you think everyone is expecting from you. It is this artificial pattern that becomes the cage, something to impress people. I would say now that I had created a golden cage studded with jewels, that they were flashing because I wanted to make an impression." She feels that treatment helped her to break the cage, that she has discarded the notions and ideas that built the cage, and that she is now free and on the outside. She takes pride in who she is, in her own goals and accomplishments, and no longer has the impulse to create an artificial superstructure. She is satisfied and content to lead her own life.